Other People

Christopher Shinn

Methuen Drama

Published by Methuen 2000

1 3 5 7 9 10 8 6 4 2

First published in Great Britain in 2000 by Methuen Publishing Limited
215 Vauxhall Bridge Road, London SW1V 1EJ

Copyright © 2000 by Christopher Shinn

The author has asserted his rights under the Copyright, Designs
and Patents Act, 1988, to be identified as the author of this work.

Methuen Publishing Limited Reg. No. 3543167

A CIP catalogue record for this book is available from the British Library.

ISBN 0 413 75220 8

Typeset by MATS, Southend-on-Sea, Essex
Printed and bound in Great Britain by
Cox & Wyman Ltd, Reading, Berkshire

Caution

ROYAL COURT

Royal Court Theatre presents

OTHER PEOPLE

by **Christopher Shinn**

First performed at the Royal Court Jerwood Theatre Upstairs,
Sloane Square, London on 17 March 2000

Supported by the American Friends of the Royal Court Theatre
and Francis Finlay

OTHER PEOPLE

by **Christopher Shinn**

Cast in order of appearance
Petra **Doraly Rosen**
Stephen **Daniel Evans**
Mark **James Frain**
Man **Nigel Whitmey**
Tan **Neil Newbon**
Darren/Waiter **Richard Cant**

Director **Dominic Cooke**
Designer **Robert Innes Hopkins**
Lighting Designer **Johanna Town**
Sound Designer **Paul Arditti**
Casting Director **Lisa Makin**
Production Manager **Sue Bird**
Company Stage Manager **Cath Binks**
Stage Management **Lara Bloomberg, Julie Sproule**
Dialect Coach **Penny Dyer**
Costume Supervisor **Suzanne Duffy**
Set Construction **Rupert Blakeley**

Royal Court Theatre wishes to thank the following for their help with this production:
Astral Club, Theatre Museum, Windmill International. Wardrobe care by Persil and Comfort courtesy of Lever Brothers Ltd.

THE COMPANY

Christopher Shinn (writer)
For the Royal Court: Four

Paul Arditti (sound designer)
Paul Arditti has been designing sound for
theatre since 1983. He currently combines his
post as Head of Sound at the Royal Court
(where he has designed more than 50
productions) with regular freelance projects.
For the Royal Court: Dublin Carol, Breath,
Boom, The Kitchen, Rat in the Skull, Some
Voices, Mojo, The Lights, The Weir. The
Steward of Christendom, Shopping and Fucking,
Blue Heart (co-productions with Out of Joint).
The Chairs (co-production with Theatre de
Complicite); The Strip, Never Land, Cleansed,
Via Dolorosa, Real Classy Affair.
Other theatre includes: Our Lady of Sligo (RNT
with Out of Joint); Some Explicit Polaroids (Out
of Joint); Hamlet, The Tempest (RSC); Orpheus
Descending, Cyrano de Bergerac, St Joan (West
End); Marathon (Gate).
Musicals include: Doctor Dolittle, Piaf, The
Threepenny Opera.
Awards include: Drama Desk Award for
Outstanding Sound Design 1992 for Four
Baboons Adoring the Sun (Broadway).

Richard Cant
Theatre: Angels in America (Manchester
Library); Hamlet, Cymbeline, Much Ado About
Nothing (RSC); The Modern Husband (ATC);
The Taming of the Shrew (Leicester Haymarket);
As You Like It (Cheek by Jowl); The Canterbury
Tales (Garrick); A Midsummer Night's Dream,
Charley's Aunt (York Theatre Royal); Love's
Labour's Lost, Dangerous Corner, The Slicing
Edge, High Society, Once in a While the Odd
Thing Happens, A View from the Bridge,
Candida (Wolsey Ipswich); Waterlands (Shaw).
Television: Privates, In a Land of Plenty, Sunburn,
Gimme, Gimme, Gimme, The Midsomer
Murders, This Life, The Day Today, Great
Expectations.
Radio: The Medieval Hitchhiker.

Dominic Cooke (director)
Associate Director of the Royal Court.
Theatre includes: As adapter and director;
Arabian Nights (Young Vic/Tour); The Marriage
of Figaro (Tour). As director; Hunting Scenes
From Lower Bavaria, The Weavers (Gate),
Afore Night Come, Entertaining Mr Sloane
(Theatr Clwyd); The Bullet (Donmar
Warehouse); My Mother Said I Never Should
(Oxford Stage Company/Young Vic); Of Mice
and Men (Nottingham Playhouse); Kiss Of The
Spiderwoman (Bolton Octagon); Autogeddon
(Edinburgh Assembly Rooms); Caravan
(National Theatre of Norway); The Importance
of Being Earnest (Atlantic Theare Festival,
Canada).
Awards include: TMA Theatre Award,
Manchester Evening News Drama Award and
Edinburgh Fringe First.
Assistant Director at the Royal Shakespeare
Company 1992-94.

Daniel Evans
For the Royal Court: Cleansed.
Theatre includes: Candide, The Merchant of
Venice, Troilus & Cressida, Peter Pan, Cardiff
East (RNT); Henry V, Coriolanus, A Midsummer
Night's Dream (RSC).
Television includes: Great Expectations, The
Case of the Private Spiers, Be Brave, Soldier,
Soldier, As You Like It, Nel, Romeo and Juliet.
Film includes: The Barber of Seville,
Chameleon, A Midsummer Night's Dream,
Mabinogi.
Radio includes: War and Peace, Wuthering
Heights, 'Gymerwch Chi Sigaret?
Awards include: Olivier nomination for Candide
(RNT).

James Frain
Theatre: Rules of the Game (Almeida), All for
Love (Almeida); She Stoops to Conquer (Peter
Hall Company); Zenobia (RSC).
Television: Arabian Nights, The Mill on the
Floss, Macbeth on the Estate, The Buccaneers,
Prime Suspect III.
Film: Hilary and Jackie, Elizabeth I, Vigo,
Rasputin, Nothing Personal, Loch Ness, An
Awfully Big Adventure, Shadowlands.
To be released Spring 2000: Where the Heart
Is, Reindeer Games, Sunshine, Titus.

Robert Innes Hopkins (designer)
Theatre includes: The Servant of Two Masters,
Comedy of Errors (RSC); Les Miserables
(Tel Aviv Arts Centre); The Tempest, Present
Laughter, The Seagull, The Wasp Factory (West
Yorkshire Playhouse); Othello (Washington
Shakespeare Theatre); My Mother Said I Never
Should (Oxford Stage Company/Tour); The
Weavers, Hunting Scenes From Lower Bavaria,
Fatzer Material (Gate Theatre); Imperfect
Librarian, Spell, Hunger (Young Vic Studio);
Happy End (Nottingham Playhouse); Miss Julie
(Young Vic); Judith (Wrestling School).
Film includes: Lucia Di Lammermoor.
Opera includes: Peter Grimes (Murnford
Theatre); Ghosts (Riverside Studios);The
Bartered Bride (Opera North); Eugene Onegin
(French Institute).
Awards include: Critics' Circle Designer of the
Year 1996 for The Weavers and Comedy of
Errors. TMA Designer of the Year 1997 for The
Wasp Factory and My Mother Said I Never
Should.

Neil Newbon
Theatre: Romeo and Juliet, They Shoot Horses
Don't They ? (Bloomsbury); Harvington Fair
(Edinburgh Festival).
Television: The Bill, Dalziel & Pascoe, London
Bridge (series III-IV), Criss Cross, Wycliffe,
Goodness Gracious Me.
To be released: Anchor Me (April 2000), Drive,
Poetic Justice.

Doraly Rosen
Theatre includes: A Respectable Trade (Bristol
Old Vic); Sunshine, Macbeth (Southwark
Playhouse); Spike Heels, Danny and the Deep
Blue Sea, Freeze Tag, Women of Manhattan,
Extremities (Flipside Studio); Modigliani (Rose
Theatre); Fool for Love, If It Ain't Good (Marilyn
Monroe).
Television includes: Casualty, The Alchemists,
Kavanagh QC.

Johanna Town (lighting designer)
Johanna has been Head of Lighting for the Royal
Court since 1990 and has designed extensively
for the company during this time. Productions
include: Toast, Choice, The Kitchen, Faith
Healer, Pale Horse, Search and Destroy,
Women Laughing, Never Land.
Other recent theatre designs include: Some
Explicit Polaroids, Drummers (Out of Joint);
Rose (RNT/Broadway); Little Malcolm
(Hampstead / West End); Our Country's Good
(Young Vic / Out of Joint); Our Lady of Sligo
(RNT / Out of Joint); Blue Heart (Royal
Court/Out of Joint/New York).
Opera Includes: Tobias and the Angel (Almeida
Opera Festival); La Boheme, Die Fledermaus
(MTL).

Nigel Whitmey
For the Royal Court: Disneyland It Ain't
Theatre includes: The Cherry Orchard,
Demons & Dybbuks, Buried Alive, Black Dahlia
(Method and Madness); Far Above Rubies
(Tricycle / Tour); Salvation (Gate); View From
the Bridge (Cheltenham Everyman); Hell's
Kitchen (Lancaster Dukes); The Revenger's
Tragedy (CTC Tour); Crossfire (Paines Plough).
Television includes: Too Much Sun, The 10th
Kingdom, Poirot, Streetwise, Lost Language of
the Cranes, The Josie Lawrence Show, Kissing
the Gunner's Daughter, Jeeves and Wooster,
Seaforth, The Paul Merton Show, Man From
Auntie, Overhere, Dark Realm.
Film includes: Jefferson in Paris, Surviving
Picasso (Merchant Ivory Productions); Saving
Private Ryan (Dreamworks); Shining Through,
Killer Tongue, Twilight of the Ice Nymphs.

THE ENGLISH STAGE COMPANY
AT THE ROYAL COURT

The English Stage Company at the Royal Court opened in 1956 as a subsidised theatre producing new British plays, international plays and some classical revivals.

The first artistic director George Devine aimed to create a writers' theatre, 'a place where the dramatist is acknowledged as the fundamental creative force in the theatre and where the play is more important than the actors, the director, the designer'. The urgent need was to find a contemporary style in which the play, the acting, direction and design are all combined. He believed that 'the battle will be a long one to continue to create the right conditions for writers to work in'.

Devine aimed to discover 'hard-hitting, uncompromising writers whose plays are stimulating, provocative and exciting'. The Royal Court production of John Osborne's Look Back in Anger in May 1956 is now seen as the decisive starting point of modern British drama, and the policy created a new generation of British playwrights. The first wave included John Osborne, Arnold Wesker, John Arden, Ann Jellicoe, N F Simpson and Edward Bond. Early seasons included new international plays by Bertolt Brecht, Eugène Ionesco, Samuel Beckett, Jean-Paul Sartre and Marguerite Duras.

The theatre started with the 400-seat proscenium arch Theatre Downstairs, and then in 1969 opened a second theatre, the 60-seat studio Theatre Upstairs. Productions in the Theatre Upstairs have transferred to the West End, such as Conor McPherson's The Weir, Kevin Elyot's My Night With Reg and Ariel Dorfman's Death and the Maiden. The Royal Court also co-produces plays which have transferred to the West End or toured internationally, such as Sebastian Barry's The Steward of Christendom and Mark Ravenhill's Shopping and Fucking (with Out of Joint), Martin McDonagh's The Beauty Queen Of Leenane (with Druid Theatre Company), Ayub Khan-Din's East is East (with Tamasha Theatre Company, and now a feature film).

Since 1994 the Royal Court's artistic policy has again been vigorously directed to finding a new generation of playwrights. The writers include Joe Penhall, Rebecca Prichard, Michael Wynne, Nick Grosso, Judy Upton, Meredith Oakes, Sarah Kane, Anthony Neilson, Judith Johnson, James Stock, Jez Butterworth, Simon Block, Martin McDonagh, Mark Ravenhill, Ayub Khan-Din, Tamantha Hammerschlag, Jess Walters, Conor McPherson, Simon Stephens, Richard

Bean, Roy Williams, Gary Mitchell, Mick Mahoney, Rebecca Gilman, Christopher Shinn and Kia Corthron. This expanded programme of new plays has been made possible through the support of the Jerwood Foundation, and many in association with the Royal National Theatre Studio.

In recent years there have been record-breaking productions at the box office, with capacity houses for Jez Butterworth's Mojo, Sebastian Barry's The Steward of Christendom, Martin McDonagh's The Beauty Queen of Leenane, Ayub Khan-Din's East is East, Eugène Ionesco's The Chairs and Conor McPherson's The Weir, which transferred to the West End in October 1998 and is now running at the Duke of York's Theatre.

The newly refurbished theatre in Sloane Square opened in February 2000, with a policy still inspired by the first artistic director George Devine. The Royal Court is an international theatre for new plays and new playwrights, and the work shapes contemporary drama in Britain and overseas.

AWARDS FOR
THE ROYAL COURT

Ariel Dorfman's Death and the Maiden and John Guare's Six Degrees of Separation won the Olivier Award for Best Play in 1992 and 1993 respectively. Terry Johnson's Hysteria won the 1994 Olivier Award for Best Comedy, and also the Writers' Guild Award for Best West End Play. Kevin Elyot's My Night with Reg won the 1994 Writers' Guild Award for Best Fringe Play, the Evening Standard Award for Best Comedy, and the 1994 Olivier Award for Best Comedy. Joe Penhall was joint winner of the 1994 John Whiting Award for Some Voices. Sebastian Barry won the 1995 Writers' Guild Award for Best Fringe Play, the 1995 Critics' Circle Award and the 1997 Christopher Ewart-Biggs Literary Prize for The Steward of Christendom, and the 1995 Lloyds Private Banking Playwright of the Year Award. Jez Butterworth won the 1995 George Devine Award for Most Promising Playwright, the 1995 Writers' Guild New Writer of the Year Award, the Evening Standard Award for Most Promising Playwright and the 1995 Olivier Award for Best Comedy for Mojo. Phyllis Nagy won the 1995 Writers' Guild Award for Best Regional Play for Disappeared.

The Royal Court was the overall winner of the 1995 Prudential Award for the Arts for creativity, excellence, innovation and accessibility. The Royal Court Theatre Upstairs won the 1995 Peter Brook Empty Space Award for innovation and excellence in theatre.

Michael Wynne won the 1996 Meyer-Whitworth Award for The Knocky. Martin McDonagh won the 1996 George Devine Award, the 1996 Writers' Guild Best Fringe Play Award, the 1996 Critics' Circle Award and the 1996 Evening Standard Award for Most Promising Playwright for The Beauty Queen of Leenane. Marina Carr won the 19th Susan Smith Blackburn Prize (1996/7) for Portia Coughlan. Conor McPherson won the 1997 George Devine Award, the 1997 Critics' Circle Award and the 1997 Evening Standard Award for Most Promising Playwright for The Weir. Ayub Khan-Din won the 1997 Writers' Guild Award for Best West End Play, the 1997 Writers' Guild New Writer of the Year Award and the 1996 John Whiting Award for East is East. Anthony Neilson won the 1997 Writers' Guild Award for Best Fringe Play for The Censor.

At the 1998 Tony Awards, Martin McDonagh's The Beauty Queen of Leenane (co-production with Druid Theatre Company) won four awards including Garry Hynes for Best Director and was nominated for a further two. Eugene Ionesco's The Chairs (co-production with Theatre de

Complicite) was nominated for six Tony awards. David Hare won the 1998 Time Out Live Award for Outstanding Achievement for Via Dolorosa. Sarah Kane won the 1998 Arts Foundation Fellowship in Playwriting. Rebecca Prichard won the 1998 Critics' Circle Award for Most Promising Playwright for Yard Gal.

Conor McPherson won the 1999 Olivier Award for Best New Play for The Weir. The Royal Court won the 1999 ITI Award for Excellence in International Theatre. Sarah Kane's Cleansed was judged Best Foreign Language Play in 1999 by Theater Heute in Germany. Rebecca Gilman won the 1999 Evening Standard Award for Most Promising Playwright for The Glory of Living.

In 1999, the Royal Court won the European theatre prize New Theatrical Realities, presented at Taormina Arte in Sicily, for its efforts in recent years in discovering and producing the work of young British dramatists.

ROYAL COURT BOOKSHOP

The bookshop offers a wide range of playtexts, theatre books, screenplays and art-house videos with over 1,000 titles.

Located in the downstairs BAR AND FOOD area, the bookshop is open Monday to Saturday, daytimes and evenings.

Many of the Royal Court Theatre playtexts are available for just £2 including the plays in the current season and recent works by Conor McPherson, Martin Crimp, Caryl Churchill, Sarah Kane, David Mamet, Phylis Nagy and Rebecca Prichard. We offer a 10% reduction to students on a range of titles.

Further information : 020 7565 5024

RE-BUILDING THE ROYAL COURT

In 1995, the Royal Court was awarded a National Lottery grant through the Arts Council of England, to pay for three quarters of a £26m project to re-build completely our 100-year old home. The rules of the award required the Royal Court to raise £7.5m in partnership funding. The building has been completed thanks to the generous support of those listed below. We are particularly grateful for the contributions of over 5,500 audience members.

If you would like to support the ongoing work of the Royal Court please contact the Development Department on 020 7565 5000.

ROYAL COURT
DEVELOPMENT BOARD
Elisabeth Murdoch (Chair)
Jonathan Cameron (Vice Chair)
Timothy Burrill
Anthony Burton
Jonathan Caplan QC
Victoria Elenowitz
Monica Gerard-Sharp
Joyce Hytner
Feona McEwan
Michael Potter
Sue Stapely
Charlotte Watcyn Lewis

PRINCIPAL DONOR
Jerwood Foundation

WRITERS CIRCLE
BSkyB Ltd
The Cadogan Estate
Carillon/Schal
News International plc
Pathé
The Eva and Hans K Rausing Trust
The Rayne Foundation
Garfield Weston Foundation

DIRECTORS CIRCLE
The Esmée Fairbairn Charitable Trust
The Granada Group plc

ACTORS CIRCLE
Ronald Cohen & Sharon Harel-Cohen
Quercus Charitable Trust
The Basil Samuel Charitable Trust
The Trusthouse Charitable Foundation
The Woodward Charitable Trust

SPECIFIC DONATIONS
The Foundation for Sport and the Arts for Stage System
John Lewis Partnership plc for Balcony
City Parochial Foundation for Infra Red Induction Loops and Toilets for Disabled Patrons
RSA Art for Architecture Award Scheme for Antoni Malinowski Wall Painting

STAGE HANDS CIRCLE
Anonymous
Miss P Abel Smith
The Arthur Andersen Foundation
Associated Newspapers Ltd
The Honorable M L Astor Charitable Trust
Rosalind Bax
Character Masonry Services Ltd
Elizabeth Corob
Toby Costin
Double O Charity
The D'Oyly Carte Charitable Trust
Thomas and Simone Fenton
Lindy Fletcher
Michael Frayn
Mr R Hopkins
Roger Jospe
William Keeling
Lex Service plc
Miss A Lind-Smith
The Mactaggart Third Fund
Fiona McCall
Mrs Nicola McFarlane
Mr J Mills
The Monument Trust
Jimmy Mulville and Denise O'Donoghue
David Murby
Michael Orr
William Poeton CBE and Barbara Poeton
Angela Pullen
Mr and Mrs JA Pye's Charitable Settlement
Ruth and Richard Rogers
Ann Scurfield
Ricky Shuttleworth
Brian Smith
The Spotlight
Mr N Trimble
Lionel Wigram Memorial Trust
Madeline Wilks
Richard Wilson
Mrs Katherine Yates

PROGRAMME SUPPORTERS

The Royal Court (English Stage Company Ltd) receives its principal funding from the Arts Council of England. It is also supported financially by a wide range of private companies and public bodies and earns the remainder of its income from the box office and its own trading activities. The Royal Borough of Kensington & Chelsea gives an annual grant to the Royal Court Young Writers' Programme and the London Boroughs Grants Committee provides project funding for a number of play development initiatives.

Royal Court Registered Charity number 231242.

This year the Jerwood Charitable Foundation continues to support new plays by new playwrights with the fifth series of Jerwood New Playwrights. Since 1993 the A.S.K. Theater Projects of Los Angeles has funded a Playwrights' Programme at the theatre. Bloomberg Mondays, a continuation of the Royal Court's reduced price ticket scheme, is supported by Bloomberg News. BSkyB have also generously committed to a two-year sponsorship of the Royal Court Young Writers' Festival. Other People is supported by The American Friends of the Royal Court Theatre and Francis Finlay.

Funded by THE ARTS COUNCIL OF ENGLAND

FOR THE ROYAL COURT

Other People

for my mother and my father

Other People premiered at the Royal Court Jerwood Theatre
Upstairs, London, on 17th March 2000.

Characters

Stephen, *mid-twenties*
Petra, *mid-twenties*
Mark, *mid-twenties*
Tan, *late teens*
Man, *thirties/forties*
Darren, *mid-twenties*

Depending upon the actor's versatility, **Darren** and **Man**
can be played by the same person; he also plays the waiter in
Act One, Scene Two.

Setting: New York City's East Village.

Act One: a few days before Christmas.
Act Two: Christmas Eve.
Act Three: New Year's Eve.

Acknowledgements
My thanks to those whose support, smarts, and inspiration
aided in the writing and initial development of this play,
especially: Tim Farrell, John Wellmann, David Greenspan,
Francine Volpe, Sonya Sobieski, Tim Sanford, Grant Varjas,
Graham Whybrow, John Belluso, Crystal Skillman and Kent
Rees.

Act One

Scene One

Hip restaurant, distant techno.

Petra People tell me this is really good, so.

Stephen Yeah?

Petra No, you look a little – I was wondering if you –

Stephen No, I'm, I guess I'm a little nervous.

Petra Yeah, you're nervous?

Stephen We talked on the phone, you know, and he sounded – he sounded – how did he sound? – he said – I don't even remember practically, I was so – nervous. We had a kind of – it was a distant conversation, he said how excited he was to leave the, you know, the clinic, and how much it meant for us to take him in, you know. He talked a little about the movie, which, Christ, the phone has been ringing off the *hook* for him, these movie people calling every half an hour – Anyway, whatever, I'm just, let's not talk about it, I'll just get more nervous. Why isn't he here yet? Let's not talk about it.

Petra Okay.
They say the food is really good, really clean food. I can eat here.

Stephen It's just this music you know.

Petra This music, yes.

Stephen You know?

Petra Well it can't be helping your nerves.

Stephen And this crowd is a little precious, look, over there – don't look, she's looking here – there, now, that's my editor, right there, in the, whatever, that incredibly boring Donna Karan – see? – the black? –

Petra   I see –

Stephen   – who assigned me four new *blurbs* to do this week because so-and-so had a family emergency, so I have to write these movie reviews now and I was supposed to not have another assignment till after – Oh wait: is this, do you hear this? – is this a techno version of *O Holy Night*? Oh, blecch!

Petra   Christmas.

Stephen   Christmas. And these waiters, hello, heil Hitler, master-race blondies, I bet they all run into each other at the same auditions.

Petra   You're very nervous, Stephen.

Stephen   I know, and I told myself I wouldn't – hearing his voice – you know – I just wish he'd get here because – there's this anxiety I mean – part of me, eight months later part of me really has forgotten even what he looks like – and to think he will go from this incredible abstract force in my memory to this physical, undeniable presence – and that – and that I don't really know him now – on the phone when we . . . I think I'll have a drink.

Petra   You're allowed to have a drink.

Stephen   Blather blather.

Petra   Can I ask you a question?

Stephen   Of course.

Petra   Are you still in love with him?

Stephen   No. *No.* I mean, I recognize, you know, we were never really in love, we were in, in *need*, or something, something passed *between* us, and it was *genuine*, but it was not – not by a long shot not – and I know that. No. But Mark and I have never really talked about – and perhaps we should have before I agreed to let him stay with us – but he sounded so – what was I going to say to him? He needs support now, after, you know, what *happened*. We'll talk about it. We'll talk about it. It'll be okay. It'll be *okay*, it

will, it just – things are – *different*. Now.
I mean, you know? I'm barely used to you being back here,
two days, and now . . .

Petra   I understand.

Stephen   Yeah . . .
You are back. Which is – wow. Go on, go, say something in
Japanese for me.

Petra   No.

Scene Two

Mark *has joined the two.*

Stephen   Because, no, listen: when you guys were away,
endless misery for the first six months, incessant, but this one
night, like less than two months ago, I had this epiphany, this
total – Can we even get some bread while we're – Mark, do
you want any bread? I'll get the waiter.

As **Stephen** *looks around, signals:*

Petra (*to* **Mark**)   I can't eat bread, the carbohydrates – they
did studies –

Stephen   These waiters, literally, it's like they're auditioning
for a Calvin Klein ad. 'Don't smile. Remove all possible
emotion from your face.'
Anyway so, this guy. The date. Cafe, nice, blah blah, we swap
stories, walk around the East Village, blab about
ex-boyfriends, look at some clothes, decide, what the hell, let's
go see a show! So we go to the half-price booth, we go to this
musical, musical's over, so we go – Darren – *Darren*'s his name
– so the show lets out, we go for a drink. Now this will sound
banal, mundane, but – we're in the bar – and I start to tell
Darren about this *grant* I'm applying for for this *play* I've
written – and by the way I'm nervous because I should be
hearing if I got this grant or not before the new year, so keep
your eye out in the mail – anyway – I tell him how I had just

gotten so frustrated with my *job* and how I'd stopped even
going on *auditions* because the stuff I was sent out for was so
wretched and so how I decided to write a *play* – you know, and
when you guys left I went back into therapy – and I'm just
beginning to really *figure out* my patterns, you know, just,
pathological sex and and this really degraded self-loathing 'love'
instinct I mean not-love but – but – I'm lonely, you know?
You guys are – I'm kind of hating my life still and – I'm really
hot for this guy actually, I mean he's *totally* – he has this weirdo
pseudo-British accent sort of, he's a musician, he's got this
really sexy, like, *detachment* going on, this really careless *swagger*
and *ambivalence* –

Petra   A million years, he tells a story.

Stephen   Okay, okay: so I tell him about the grant and the
play and he says he wants to read it. 'I'd really like to read it,
Stephen. Sounds totally cool.' But I feel – I feel *weird*. I feel
something's off here. Because – and I realize – I turn around
briefly because I realize something about his *gaze* – he's not
quite looking at me, he's sort of just looking *above* me, above
my shoulder, and he's been fixed there the whole – and so I
look behind me and I see that – and my heart – *breaks* – I see
that he's watching the TV – above the bar. As he's talking to
me. The – so I say, 'Derek? Derek?' And he says, 'Hold on'.

Petra   Darren or Derek his name is?

Stephen   He, whatever – 'Hold on'. And it's not – the show
is like Entertainment Tonight but not, it's like a *lighter* version
of Entertainment Tonight, they're interviewing some *blonde*
woman, some sitcom, and I turn back around and I start to
say something else you know and he says, 'One more sec'. *One
more sec.*
And. And so. I mean that's it.

Petra   So the story ends you went to bed with him.

Stephen   No! No he asked me to go home with him and I
just said – 'Not tonight but I'll call' or whatever. Because, you
know, because I *saw* at that moment – I understood – I
thought: *how many of the people I've slept with have actually looked at*

me? And I decided no, I decided, I will not go to bed with anyone for the rest of my *life* whom I do not perceive has at the very least an *interest in me as a human being.* You know, as a separate person.

Because – you know? There I am, sitting before him, a real – TV – me – and he picks – because *no.* Because that will not be my life. Anymore.

Where's the bread? The service here, seriously, it's like service with an ironic smile. It's a postmodern restaurant, like, the waiters are just actors acting the role of waiters but really aren't waiters and if you were hip enough to understand it you'd enjoy yourself.

You're not going home for Christmas, are you Petra?

Petra   No, oh no, my parents think I'm still in Japan and I'm not about to – so if they call, you know, don't –

Stephen   Yeah, I'm not going home either, first time too, this year I am standing *up* for myself. Because it would be self-loathing to go back there. My play I'm working on, it's actually about, it's about these certain events, this thing that happened in my hometown, this really, this *beautiful* and *devastating* thing actually – but – I'll tell you about it but – I'm talking a lot. What about you Mark? What are you doing for Christmas?

Mark   I'll be here.

Pause.

Stephen   Well. Well then we are going, we are going to have a fabulous Christmas I've decided.

Petra   I'm glad you decided that, ha.

Stephen   We will!

Petra   I know, I know, I'm just teasing.

Waiter *drops a basket of bread on the table.*

Petra   Well.

Stephen   Bravo.

Stephen *reaches for the bread.*

Mark   Can we say grace first?

Stephen *and* **Petra** *look at* **Mark**.

Mark   I'd like to say grace.

Stephen   I think it'd be a first for this place. We're in Dante's fifth ring and you want to say grace.

Mark *bows his head.*

Mark   God, bless you for this food before us, and bless those less fortunate, those in pain, those in hunger, those in need of your beauty and your bounty. Amen.

Petra/Stephen   Amen.

A beeper goes off. **Mark** *checks, shuts it off. He takes a piece of bread.* **Stephen** *follows.* **Petra** *sips water.*

Scene Three

Apartment. SR living room, homemade wall center, SL **Stephen***'s bedroom, far right wall is small kitchen unit, hall off leading to* **Petra***'s bedroom, upstage of kitchen unit is door leading to tiny bathroom and shower.*

Living room: a couch, a bookshelf, coffee table, small entertainment system.

Stephen*'s bedroom: loft-bed, small desk, boxes.*

Windows SR look out on street, SL windows look out on brick.

Lights rise on **Stephen** *on his loft-bed,* **Mark** *on the couch on the phone.* **Petra** *emerges from her room, bundled up in a long coat.*

Mark   – well yeah. I can come in, well. Um. You should.

Petra *exits the apartment.* **Stephen** *looks up from his bed.*

Mark   Well like I said I'll have to. Oh? Well I suppose this is all. Great, especially for. Well I can come in I can. Anytime.

Okay. That's fine. But like I said. Till I see it. Okay. Yeah. Till
I. Well that's great that people are. But like I said. Okay. Okay
that's fine. Okay. Bye.

He hangs up the phone. He opens up a book. **Stephen** *climbs off his
loft-bed, grabs his coat from the closet, enters the living room.*

Stephen   Hey.

Mark   Oh. Hi.

Stephen   Hey thanks again for dinner.

Mark   Oh. You're welcome but. I have all this money.

Stephen   Yeah. I was gonna – oh, whatcha reading?

Mark   The Bible.

Stephen (*laughs*)   Ha. (*Stops.*) Oh – The Bible, really?

Mark   The Good Book.

Stephen   The Good News Bible.

Mark   The King James version.

Stephen   Right. Right. Um. Well I was going to go down to
the deli and get myself a Snapple or – how are you feeling,
you want anything . . .?

Mark   I'm fine.

Stephen   Snapple has this new peach juice which is –
anyway, I'm just, I'm just going to say this however foreign to
my nature it is to speak *directly, honestly,* you know, but, that's
one of the things I've been working on, so. So. I just: I want to
know you're okay. I guess. You've been really quiet, and . . .

Mark   I'm fine. Really. I know I'm. I know this is. Different.
Unlikely even.

Stephen   Well yeah! Very – it's definitely a – *new you* here,
ha.

Mark   With the help of the Lord, yes. A new. Me.

Pause.

Stephen   I'm just, I'm a little uneasy, it's been so long you know and I feel a little – *lost* with you – and of course, our history, you know, and – your coming back here without our discussing – what's really *happened* in the – in the time you've been – gone – *you* – you not being something we've discussed and why – when you could stay anywhere why – I mean I knew it was a rough time so I didn't want to push but – now – just to know – what's going through your head . . .

Mark   Right. Well. I think you'll find I tend to be more – silent and not. Interested. In the past. Because. It causes me pain to think about it. My life is about. The new me. In so many ways. In this way (*Holds up the Bible.*) especially.

Stephen   Right. Right, well. And that's great, that's what you needed to – recover. And I understand, I guess I'm just being selfish, you know... Petra's the same way: she was in Japan for over half a year, you know, stripping, and she's finally given it up, you know, she saved a lot of money and she's come back so now she has money to write and to – do what she wants without having to – you know, and which is *great* – and she's the same, not wanting to – *talk,* to *define* herself based on – so. So. It's hard for *me* but I understand.

Mark   The past is – bad news. It's only good news now. For me. And thank God. Thank God.

Stephen   Right, sure. It's just so – different.

But – well – hell you know – maybe we're all – getting it together, which is great. Like our apartment is about *health* you know, *healthy* living – we're all – being *proactive* – not to sound not to sound New Agey but . . .

Mark   You don't sound New Agey.

Stephen   Right, well, we're making *improvements.*

Mark   Absolutely. God bless us. It's not easy. This world.

Stephen   Yeah! Yeah, and I guess, and it doesn't have to be now, I guess though I just hope we will you know eventually have a chance to *talk,* really *talk,* about the past

year and – you know? Just to – and – well maybe I thought –
I'd feel better if I – if we – hugged, I mean we haven't –.
Because – I do love you, not, not in the past way but in this
new way, you know?

Mark Change is traumatic. It will take getting used to. The
past me, Stephen. That's someone else. Have faith in. This
me. Have faith in me now and know all will. Will be alright.

Stephen Right.

Mark I'll give you a hug.

Stephen Good.

Mark *stands, hugs* **Stephen** *briefly, breaks the hug.*

Mark You're my only friend. Only true, real friend in this
world. I was too terrified to go at it alone, to jump back into
the. Real world. Without you. God bless you. I say prayers of
thanks that I am here with you.

Stephen Right, right, well great.

The phone rings.

Mark Oh, give me some peace! Let the voice-mail get it.

Stephen Who are these, are these the movie people?

Mark Yes. Oh Stephen. I have the option – because most
of what was used ended up being mine – of putting my name
on the film. Which I haven't – seen. This is. A dilemma.

Stephen Oh.

Mark They're sending me the cut. It doesn't really matter.
The Lord will guide me.

Stephen Right. Um – well I have to get going on these
blurbs I – I hope I didn't – upset you or – I just get neurotic,
still, I hate it.

Mark Then give it up. Release yourself to the Holy Spirit.
What's 'neurotic'? What is that? Hand it to God, he'll know
what to do with it. It won't be easy. But you can do it.

Stephen   Yeah. Yeah. God, it's a Marianne Williamson moment! Right – well – you're probably right. I'm just – so proud of you. And Petra. And glad you'll be getting to know each other, I always kept you two apart, I kept my life so compartmentalized before, you know.
Well I'll let you get back to your reading. God, when I was a kid, I was into this totally weird Wiccan stuff. – Anyway. You want anything from the deli?

Mark   I don't need anything.

Stephen   Okay.

Stephen *goes to the door.*

Um. And just – anytime you need anything. *Anything.* I am here for you.

Mark   Thank you.

Stephen   Anything at all. Just knock on my door. Anytime no matter what. I want you to be well.

Mark   I will be. And God bless you.

Stephen   Right. Okay. Just – wanted to say that. So. Off to get my Snapple!

Stephen *goes.* **Mark** *opens the Bible.*

Scene Four

Petra, *in a red gown, sits at a small table with a* **Man**. *Music. Drinks.*

Petra   Oh now, this is fantasy.

Man   Petra, I swear to God. During office hours. Countless girls. Sliding their leg against mine or… hiking up their – literally coming onto me like I can't tell you. It was this basic business class I was teaching. Yeah.

Petra   No, I don't believe you, no: countless?

Man   Are you in college?

Petra   No.

Man   Graduate.

Petra   Yes.

Man   Where did you go to school?

Petra   Twenty questions we're playing here.

Man   Okay. What was your major?

Petra   Clearly, I mean, you're smiling like something's going on in that brain of yours, so what are you getting at?

Man   Well, you're smart, you're perceptive, maybe I've a little theory I'm working on. Acting?

Petra   Oh God please, say anything but that.

Man   Well then. No. Okay. But you did this to pay for school, you danced?

Petra   I had a scholarship, a very substantial scholarship, but not nearly enough to live on, and I knew that this was the only thing I could –

Man   Creative writing.

Petra   Who have you been talking to? Which girl? Joanna?

Man   Joanna, no. Joanna gives handjobs.

Petra   I don't.

Man   Whoa! I didn't ask you if you did, I wasn't asking you to, I was telling you, No, I don't care to talk to Joanna. I like you. I want to hear you talk about your interesting life. I say that without irony. I mean it: you, you are interesting to me.

Petra   Listen, I had a poetry professor at NYU –

Man   Ahh, NYU girl.

Petra   – no, listen: National Book Award this man won, and constantly, *constantly* asked me out to have 'beer' with him, a 'beer'. I said I don't drink. Said why don't we go 'work out' together. You believe this? Oh, no, I don't work out I say. Office hours: tells me my poems give him *erections*. Tells me he graded my poems, hands me the paper says, see this, this is my cum on your poems, guess I gotta give you an A plus. I am – I am eighteen years old, I am from Queens, my father doesn't barely know how to *write* or *read* and here is Mr. National Book Award . . . and my father was a decent man, he was – he was the kind of man who calls radio call-in shows and says I'm a white man and I can tell you that whites are still racist against blacks. So I know this is wrong, this man is *wrong*. But I am stunned and can barely move – I am smiling – I have no idea what to *say*. So he makes a joke, whatever, and I say, okay, and I gotta go, and I get an A plus in the class. And I'm eighteen years old. So you're telling me girls are pulling up their *skirts* and – no. And if this is so, this is depressing.

Man   See, the class I taught was a night class and maybe those girls tend to be more desperate. But hey, I always said no. I did.

So if you stripped to get through school, and you went over to Japan and made a lot of money, what uh, why are you doing it now? What's the reason now?

Petra   Well, what do *you* think? Why don't *you* tell me. Ha.

Man   No, no, I know I've been talking a lot. But I really want to know from you.

Pause.

Petra   Listen, I'm sorry, I'm just a little uncomfortable here, I think maybe you should talk with one of the other girls.

Man   No, please. Here.

He puts down a fifty dollar bill on the table.

Please.

She stops for a moment. Then goes, off.

Scene Five

The apartment. Dark. **Mark** *sits on his couch-bed, under covers, the phone pressed to his ear. Door opens,* **Petra** *enters, tired.* **Mark** *hangs up the phone, door slams shut.*

Mark (*quietly*)   Hey.

Petra   Oh, I didn't wake you up, did I?

Mark   No. I baked some cookies, couldn't sleep. Want one?

Petra   Oh, I don't eat carbohydrates or sugar.

Mark   I'm sorry.

Petra   Me too, ha. But sugar, I think it makes you depressed, it's not widely known. And carbohydrates turn to sugar – so I'm doing an experiment of cutting it out.

Mark   Good for you, Petra.

Petra   But, I have this job interview in the morning so I should go to sleep. Stephen asleep?

Mark   Before you go to sleep, I made you this.

He hands her a card.

Petra   Oh, you made this yourself?

Mark   I just wanted to let you know how much I appreciate your allowing me to stay here. How blessed I feel.

Petra   Oh, how sweet. Oh, thank you.

Mark   So. Goodnight.

Petra   Well, goodnight to you too. I hope it's warm enough in here.

Mark   It is. Hey.

Mark *stands and walks over to* **Petra**, *gives her a big hug.*

Petra   Oh.

A few more seconds and the hugs breaks.

Mark   Thank you.

Petra   You're so sweet. Thank you again for the card. It's beautiful.

Mark *goes back to the couch.*

Petra   Goodnight.

Mark   Goodnight. And hey. Good for you, Petra.

Petra (*stops, turns*)   What?

Mark   Good for you for quitting stripping.

Scene Six

East Village street. **Mark** *sits with pad, sketching.* **Tan**, *late teens, sees* **Mark**, *watches.* **Tan** *is dressed in old jeans, a long-sleeve T-shirt, and a wool hat.*

Tan   Hey, got a smoke?

Mark *turns.*

Mark   Sorry, I don't smoke.

Tan   No? Wow. 'Cuz you look like you do.

Mark   Sorry.

Mark *turns back to sketching.*

Tan   So why not me?

No response. **Tan** *moves closer, laughs.*

I mean, hey, people in a coffee-house, three o'clock, artists, musicians, whatever man. Sitting smoking blah blah blah you know? Why draw that? I mean how interesting are *they?* That's shit, you know? That's like – a bowl of fruit – or my asshole – would be a better subject.

Mark *smiles politely, continues to sketch.*

Tan *lights a cigarette.* **Mark** *looks.*

Tan   It's my last one.
Whatever.
You want one?

Mark   I told you.

Tan   Yeah, I know what you told me.

Pause.

'Kay then. Hey you wanna make a bet?

Mark   A bet.

Tan   I bet you ten bucks I can guess what brand of underwear you got on.

Mark   Ha, I don't uh –

Tan   Bet it's Calvin Klein.

Beat.

Mark   You're wrong.

Tan   I guess I owe you ten bucks. I don't got it though. Hey if you can't guess what kind I'm wearing we'll be even. Wanna find out?

Mark   No.

Beat. **Tan** *lifts up his shirt, reveals underwear sticking up out of his jeans.*

Tan   Fruit of the Loom!

Scene Seven

Late lunch. Midtown restaurant.

Petra   You know: *What was your major? Oh have I read anything of yours? Oh my daughter just graduated from law school and she wrote a legal thriller kind of a John Grisham except a female version.*

Stephen   Brilliant.

Petra Then he asks me what I write. So I think – so I decide to tell him, who knows, I think, don't judge, okay?, maybe he really cares. So I say, so I say: 'I write about the dynamics of working class-communities, the sexual violence of childhood, power dynamics between children and adults' – you know, I give him the spiel. And he nods and says: *So why does this job interest you Patricia?*

Stephen Mmm-hmmm.

Petra So barely an hour ago this is, I still feel two feet tall. So I say, Look – I'm very blunt – I say, 'I'm looking to work in a positive, stable environment, where I feel supported, where my work is appreciated, where there's a sense of structure,' and I say, and I *say*, 'Because this sense of structure has been missing from my life.' So he asks about the missing year and I lie and say I've been waitressing and he says, *Ahh, starving artist.* And then he says, *It says here you type forty words a minute.* I nod. *Well fifty-five is required for the job.* Oh. I nod. Because? – you know? And he says: *Do you know Powerpoint? Do you know Excel? Do you know Quark?* No. No. No. And then! Then: *I actually majored in literature for about a year as an undergraduate, do you believe that?* And he's laughing; and I'm *not* laughing. I say Yes. Yes I do believe that. Because I will not let him know I feel *humiliated.* Because I will have *dignity* even if – and he says *Well* and they'll be in touch and on and on and then I'm on the street.

Stephen Well I'm just – it's enough to make you want to go back to stripping.

Petra Well I won't do that. (*Beat.*) I mean, I dressed appropriately, right?

Stephen Yes! God, I am so far behind in these blurb reviews, I have to get back.

Petra Right.

Stephen I mean I have a few more minutes but. Who are these people? Oh – my boss wants to see me at four, who knows what that's about.

Petra   Well, I try to count my blessings but – I can't believe you're eating that burger.

Stephen   I know, it's disgusting, isn't it.
I wonder what Mark's doing right now.

Petra   He's a sweetheart, Stephen.

Stephen   Yeah – but this Bible stuff. Whoa, you know.

Petra   It bothers you?

Stephen   No, it's okay I mean – but – I just feel like we haven't . . . yeah, I mean, of *course* it bothers me – The Lord will provide? But. But I've never been addicted to crack, so. So what do I know. I mean, is he even sleeping with men anymore? I dunno, I just feel like I don't – those missing months where I have no *idea* – I mean I understand *why* – oh I dunno, I'm just nervous really about this grant which I should be hearing about but – I wish we had more time, I feel so rushed, it's so hard to connect like this, you know, but: well what are you doing tonight?

Petra   Oh, I'm seeing some old girlfriends really late – Christmassy thing. After this I'm gonna go to the library before it closes.

Stephen   Well we'll catch up. Hey have you seen *Men in Black*?

Petra   No.

Stephen   No. Oh well. I sort of like Will Smith.

(*Picking up check.*) Christ, I have to stop this, my bank account is fucked.

Petra   Yeah, Will Smith's very charming. They love him in Japan.

Stephen   Yeah, yeah, he's good.

Scene Eight

The apartment. **Tan** *sits on the couch, reads a magazine.* **Mark** *sits at the table with his pad.*

Tan   'How to Get and Keep a Man in Your Bed.' People
live like this?

Mark   I don't know.

Tan   'Bulimia's Grip.'

'Erection Myths.'

'AIDS and Women: The Unreported Risks.'

'Leonardo DiCaprio Loves His Mom.' Fuck, I'm cuter than
Leonardo DiCaprio, he has *no* muscle. *Cosmopolitan* bullshit. I
partied with him once, what a *dork*.
So a chick lives here. I hope.

Tan *grabs remote, turns on TV. MTV.*

Man this song *bites*. Fucking poseurs. Man this world is just full
of fucking *poseurs*.

Mark   Could you turn that off.

Tan   What?

Mark   I just. I like to control what I. Expose myself to.

Tan   You mean you don't like MTV.

Mark   Well. Sort of.

Tan   'Kay.

He shuts it off.

So what's the rent here?

Mark   I think it's seventeen-fifty.

Tan   Whoo-hoooo! Rip off!

So.

So look I'm waiting for you to take your dick out and it's been
like half an hour and I'm getting a little nervous.

Mark *laughs.*

Tan   I'm not a hustler.

Mark   I should hope you're not. I didn't expect that you were.

Tan   I mean, are you waiting for me to – I thought we were having sex. I mean, I want to.

Mark   I'm not interested in sex.

Tan   You mean with me or in general? I mean, I'm not stupid, you know, I mean, if I was a fat kid I don't think this is where I'd be right now.

Mark   I don't want to go to bed with you.

Tan   There's only one thing I do for money. I have a specialty. What are you doing?

Mark   I'm working on my sketch.

Tan   Thing I do I'm famous for is I jerk off on the street. Bare-assed, you know, bare *feet*, not a thing on, just me and my shit. In public, anywhere – it costs a lot because of the risk involved. When a guy tries to pick me up that's what I say, I say I do one thing and it costs three hundred bucks but you've never seen anyone do anything like it and you never will again.

Mark   Sounds dangerous.

Tan   I don't have to touch the guy, he doesn't touch me, we're outside. I do it wherever, depending on the time of day and stuff. Never got arrested either.

Do you mind if I just jerk off for myself? You can just watch. (*Smiles.*) No charge.

Mark   If you want to do that, you should leave.

Tan   So why would you draw people in a coffee-house, artists and shit? That's boring. What are you?

Mark   What am I? I . . . am a filmmaker.

Tan   Oh yeah? You make movies?

Mark   I made one.

Tan   Huh.

I know famous people. I told you I partied with Leonardo DiCaprio, dude is *soft*.

So um if you like to control what you expose yourself to why'd you invite me over?

Mark   Look. You can leave, I mean. You're free to do whatever you want. I'm not here to. Do anything. To. I just thought. I thought I was being kind. I thought I would show you some kindness.

Tan   Yeah, what's that line, I have always depended on the kindness of strangers or whatever. Cool movie. Ha. Well I can take a day off from busting my nut, fuck, it's the Christmas season. *O holy niiiiight* . . .

Mark   That's my favorite Christmas song.

Tan   Yeah, I bet you like that part *fallll on your kneeees*. Ha. Right.
Okay. I got. What do I got.

Tan *takes a plastic baggie of pills out from his pocket, lays it on table.*

These are not cheap either because these are good, just so you know. I got three Valium – I crush 'em up and snort 'em, you absorb it quicker that way . . . a few Quaaludes. I have these things, basically they're like prescription strength Motrin, they're not opiate based so basically they're just for if you have a very bad headache. I have Marinol, that's like synthetic THC, they're cool, these little brown liquid capsules, I know this guy who has cancer and gets these by the barrel from the government but all he wants to do is smoke pot so I trade him bags for this stuff. Got some black tar from a friend out west. Couple Vicodin . . .
So.

Mark   I am a recovering drug addict.

Tan   Oh.
Wow. Recovering, does that mean . . .

Mark   It means I've been sober for five months.

The door opens. Christmas tree. **Stephen** *enters behind tree.* **Tan** *puts the drugs away.*

Stephen   I got a treee-eee! I got a treee-eee!

Stephen *sees.*

Oh. Hi.

Mark   That's a beautiful tree.

Stephen   Well, I have to take the wires off, we'll see then. Of course it's too big and there's no space but I figured if we're going to have a beautiful Christmas we need a beautiful tree.
Hi, I'm Stephen.

Tan   Hey. Yeah, there's nothing fucking worse than X-mas in New York.

Mark   Stephen, this is Tan.

Stephen   Tan? Tan's a – where did you get that name, it's great.

Tan (*standing*)   Yeah man, Mark invited me over to take a shower, I thought he was weird or something but he's, like, the Pope, so. City's driving me crazy, man! The *music* – BLAH BLAH BLAH, BLAH BLAH BLAH, BLAH BLAH ALL THE WAY – ha! – yeah – you know – and people aren't happy. Couple days they'll be like joining *gyms* and buying the *patch* and shit.

Stephen   Right. Well, only a few more days of that I guess, so you'll survive. Anyway – I'll just dig up the ornaments and maybe, all of us, we can decorate the tree. I bought some Christmas music too, cheapo cassettes from the Duane Reade, and uhh – alcohol-free egg nog.

He pulls the tapes and the egg nog from the bag and puts them on the kitchen counter.

The ornaments and the lights and stuff are somewhere in my room, so.

He goes into his room. Throughout the following, we see him looking around his cluttered room for decorations.

Tan   He cool?

Mark   Sorry?

Tan   What's he do?

Mark   He writes . . . movie reviews for an online magazine.

Tan   Cool. You two uhh . . . ?

Mark   No.

Tan   Cool. Hey you know, look, I'm just – I'm not a squatter, okay, I have my own place, I support myself.

Mark   Yes?

Tan   I left home you know because my parents – and school – and me being – all that shit. But I don't want you to think I'm some, like, street-kid poseur 'cuz I'm *not*, some fucking –

Mark   Okay.

Tan   Yeah. So. (*Beat.*) I wanna kiss you man. You're sweet. You're weird.

Mark   You can't kiss me.

Tan   Why not?

Stephen *enters with a box.*

Stephen   Here we go.

Hey, was there anything in the mail for me today?

Mark   Just *The Nation*.

Stephen   Right. Well. Let's take a look!

Stephen *undoes the wires; the tree spreads out.*

Tan   Hey I think I'll take that shower now.

Mark   All right.

Tan *goes into the bathroom.* **Stephen** *looks at the tree. The shower turns on behind the door.* **Stephen** *turns to* **Mark**.

Stephen   Hey.

Mark   Hi.

Stephen *puts ornaments onto the couch.*

Mark   I feel as though you're upset with me.

Stephen   No – no. This is your home. My home is . . .

Mark   I thought a shower. He was so. Obviously hungry and I was reminded of. I guess he reminded me of – myself and. Clearly this is someone who's been shown no love, and – it seemed like the Christian thing to do.

Stephen   I'm just surprised all your Bible talk didn't scare him off.

Mark   What does that mean?

Stephen   Nothing – I don't mean – anything.

Mark   And I thought, Well maybe I should show some discretion but. But why show discretion because. Because of how we're taught to treat. People. Because how we treat them sometimes – makes them what they are.

Stephen   Absolutely.

Mark   Good.

Pause.

Stephen   So this is the part where you ask about my day.

Mark   I'm sorry. How was your day?

Stephen *starts to put a few decorations on the tree.*

Stephen   They did not like, listen to this, they did not like my *blurbs*, my blurbs were rejected, two of the four because, they said, they used words like brisk and *self-assured* as being qualities my blurbs did not *have*, you know, meaning, these are not *arch* enough, – straight-faced, I'm sitting in the office, I'm

nervous actually nervous, and, and have you noticed this trend
among women, this trend where they do not *like* homosexual
men, I mean I know that's a dangerous generality but she said,
These are too *soft*, these lack *punch*, I mean, she might as well
have said I don't have the *balls* to write a blurb of *Men In Black*.
So. So now I have to rewrite the blurbs and it's like, look, I
don't want to go back to temping, which was which was *soul-
murder*, which was pure degradation every hour on the hour,
and I don't certainly do not want to 'bartend' again and it's
getting to the point where it's like – I mean I'm not gonna
move where would I *move* Los Angeles? and it's – but what can
I do to make money that will not take all my energy and
slowly and utterly *kill* me because I have been there before,
you know, Huck Finn, 'I've been there before,' and, you
know, he's off floating on a raft and happy and won't be
civilized and of course he won't go back, he's a bright guy, but
then, you know, Mark Twain wrote the book, not Huck
Finn –

Apartment buzzer.

Well. Saved by the buzzer just as I was getting incoherent. But
I am, I'm enraged, and am I *wrong*, you know, am I *indulgent*,
well I say *No* because that's what they want me to think so I'll
shut up and be a good little – (*Pushing intercom button.*) Hello?

Petra (*off*)   Hi I need help down here.

Stephen   Help?

Petra (*off*)   Come down.

Stephen   Okay.

He lets go of buzzer. Looks at **Mark**.

I hope everything's okay.

Stephen *goes.* **Tan** *emerges from bathroom, not wet, shower running.
He's wrapped in a towel.*

Tan   Where'd whats-his-name go?

Mark   Downstairs for a moment. Is something wrong?

Tan   Well the water pressure was bitching which shocked me so I should have known something was wrong. Um. It just wouldn't get hot. You know. Or even warm. It's ice.

Mark *looks away.*

Tan   Everything okay?

Mark   Yeah.

Tan   Okay. Hey, can I borrow some underwear?

Mark   Sure.

Mark *goes to a bag, gets underwear, hands them to* **Tan**.

Tan   Calvin Klein. Cool.

So why'd you invite me here, for real.

Mark   I've told you. (*Beat.*) I bought some pie this morning. Would you like a piece?

Tan   Pie?

Mark   Apple pie.

Tan   Whatever.

Tan *goes back into the bathroom. Shower cuts off. Door opens. A tree.*

Stephen   Surprise!

They enter, with the tree, which is smaller than the first.

Petra   I had no idea. Ridiculous, can you believe it?

Stephen   It's a great New York story.

Petra   Two trees we have.

Stephen   I told Petra this'd be our affirmative action tree – we'll put Kwanzaa and Hanukkah ornaments on it.

Petra   Don't forget Solstice, people are getting into this whole Solstice thing.

Stephen *puts the tree in an opposite corner, sets it against the wall.*

Petra   I wanted to cheer myself up because of this interview, so I bought it.

Mark   Petra, do you want a piece of pie?

Petra   Pie?

Mark   Apple p – that's right, the –

Petra (*laughs*)   – no carbs.

Mark   How about it, Stephen. Let's have some pie.

Stephen   Well – all right.

Petra   Oh, the best part I didn't tell you, the best part was how the guy kept telling me how skinny I was, at the interview, during, and finally he goes and comes back with a bagel. He says, You're going to eat this, and then I had to explain the whole no-carb thing to him.

Stephen   This no-carb thing sounds like a cult.

Tan *comes out of the bathroom, fully-dressed.*

Tan   Hey.

Stephen   Hey Tan. We have two trees to decorate now. You wanna help?

Tan   I actually have a thing to go to, so, you know how it is.

Mark   You're leaving?

Stephen   Tan, this is Petra, Petra, Tan.

Petra   Hello.

Tan   Hey. Yeah, so. Hey, thanks for the underwear.

Mark   You're welcome.

Tan   Yeah . . .
Fuck, I'm looking for a jacket, I'm realizing I don't have one! Stupid!

Stephen   Oh, you should have a coat.

Tan   Whatever, global warming, El Niño, I'm okay.

Stephen   I'm sure I have a coat you can take.

Tan   I don't know, will it match my sensibility? Ha.

Stephen   Well . . .

Petra   I have a man's hat you're welcome to take.

Tan   Got a hat.

Takes it from his pocket, throws it on. **Stephen** *grabs long gray overcoat from closet.*

Stephen   Here, I don't wear this.

Tan   Really?

He takes it, puts it on.

Cool, I look like a dirty old man, like a flasher or somebody.

He 'flashes' and laughs.

Okay, merry X-mas, joy on earth, peace to the world, all that shit. (*'Bye.'*) Bah!

Stephen   Bye.

Mark   Bye, Tan.

He goes. A moment.

Petra   So . . . who was that?

Stephen   Friend of Mark's. He was struck by the Christmas spirit and offered a streetboy a place to shower.
He seems like a nice kid.

Mark   He is.

Stephen   That's sad.

Mark   He said the water didn't get hot.

Stephen   The shower? Really?

Stephen *goes into the bathroom. Shower cuts on.* **Mark** *goes, off.*

Petra   How was your day, Mark?

Mark (*off*)   I did a sketch today. How was your day?

Petra   I suppose it could have been worse.

Mark (*off*)   That's a good attitude to have.

Stephen *returns.*

Stephen   Hot water's fine.

Mark *returns with a piece of pie on a plate and a fork.*

Mark   Huh.

Stephen   Maybe he didn't know how to turn it on or something.

Mark (*laughs*)   Well, I'm sure that wasn't it, it's a knob.

Stephen   Well – okay. Well maybe you're right. Maybe he didn't want to take a shower, how's that. So – tonight we decorate? Petra?

Petra   Oh, remember tonight I'm going out with some old girlfriends? And I have to find some time to read tonight, I'm behind in my reading.

Stephen   Okay. Well we'll find a time we can all do it. Mark, maybe we'll go to a movie. I was telling Mark they rejected my blurbs today.

Petra   Oh, really?

Stephen   Yeah, I don't want to talk about it.

Petra   Well, I am going to take a little nap I think.

Stephen   Okay.

Petra *goes.*

Stephen   So. Movie.

Mark   Actually, you know. This will sound – odd, but. I don't go to movies anymore.

Stephen   Oh.

Mark   It just. I like to control what I. Expose myself to.

Stephen   Well not every movie is directed by Quentin Tarantino.

Mark   I know that.

Here.

Hands **Stephen** *a plate of pie, with fork, goes off.*

Mark (*off*)   Yeah, I think I'll just read and take a shower and get to bed early tonight.

Stephen *goes to couch, sits.*

Stephen   Okay. Well. Well maybe it's the perfect time to finish my Christmas shopping. I just figured out what I'm going to get you.

Mark (*off*)   Walking around today, it was quite amazing to see how a religious holiday has become such an excuse for rampant consumerism!

Stephen   Right –

Mark *returns with a bottle of water.*

Stephen   Well maybe tonight after I shop we'll just hang out and talk, we can talk –

Stephen *takes a bite of pie.* **Mark** *goes to the couch, sits.*

Mark   I'll be asleep when you get back most likely.

Stephen (*chewing*)   Oh, right.
Where's your piece?

Mark   I'm not having one.

Stephen   – Oh.

Mark *smiles. As does* **Stephen**. **Mark** *takes a sip of water.* **Stephen** *swallows his bite of pie.*

Scene Nine

Strip club. **Petra** *with the same* **Man** *as before.*

Petra   Before he died, then, you actually knew him.

Man   I used to go to this diner all the time he worked at, you know, by where I live, the show was going up, we were all real excited for him – he was just our waiter, at the time.

Petra   Wow.

Man   Do you like it? You've seen it?

Petra   I have.

Man   You said you lived in the East Village, so I –

Petra   No, I understand.

Man   I mean, you're not – perhaps I'm being dumb, or presumptuous, I mean, what do I know? . . .

Petra   You're not being dumb.

Man   But you don't like the show, or . . . ? The critics, they liked it, people, people seem to – standing ovation the night I saw it – Pulitzer Prize. So I'm interested in why, if – isn't that – East Village – but – why don't you talk.

Petra   Look – thirteen-year-old kids, fat girls, gay boys, they love it, so. I don't, truly, I don't think about it. No. If I did think about it I would get angry because. Because it's another example of. It's – *condescending*.

Man   How is that?

Petra   Because. Because I work hard and. I work to try to be an *artist* – which, it's an embarrassment to even use that word –

Man   Why?

Petra   Listen – I read. I work hard. And what the show says to me is – is am I indecent, or, or am I 'selling out' or am I *inauthentic* because I want, I want money or, or an apartment which is even just *decent*? I mean when do any of those characters read? What are they doing with all their time, I don't – and we *celebrate* these people, and don't get me wrong, everyone is *valuable*, but, but *what* are we celebrating?

Man   Life. The artistic life. Refusal to compromise. Right?

Petra   Wanna know who lives in the East Village? A lot of the actors in the show that's who. Those characters, it's like Peter Pan Neverland, refusal to grow up, join the real – I know it's a *musical* but – it avoids asking any real, I mean, *genuine* questions and instead makes – makes a mockery of – my roommate said this and I agree – makes a *spectacle* of AIDS, gays, lesbians, blacks – it – *commodifies* actual – and tell me these people who are in it and who directed it have no idea how they're mocking themselves and their – their own *choices* – oh whatever.

Man   No, no, please, this is! – You're . . . how can I say this . . . threatened then. By these characters.

Petra   Well.

What I was going to say was. I'm not used to having to think too hard when I'm here.

Man   Change the subject then. I want to hear one of your poems.

Petra   Oh come on.

Man   Why are you embarrassed? My goodness, the fact that you write poems – is fascinating to me! Would you tell me one?

Petra   I, they're written down, so.

Man   See, you are just – who you are – comes through and is – fascinating! So. So I know this isn't – I'm not stupid –

He takes out his wallet.

I'm under no –

He puts money on the table.

There. For a poem. For one poem.

Petra   I'll talk to you but. No.

Man   Okay. Okay. We talk. Here: I just saw this movie? *Boogie Nights?* What did you think of it?

Petra   All those movies, *Trainspotting, Boogie Nights,* Quentin Tarantino, I – I can't.

Man   Can't . . . ? You don't . . . obviously don't –

Petra   It's immoral because – I live in *this world* and – they – they romanticize – and *ignore* – what – they leave out of this experience, this, being alive – and I think: is this what I must include? To be *valued?* Rewarded? *Depravity?* To be seen must I write what is more or less – more or less *pornography*, something that *titillates* with violence and sex? Or else – *My Best Friend's Wedding* and *The Celestine Prophecy* and *The Bridges of Madison County?* Do you see?

Man   I come here you know.

Petra   You . . . ?

Man   You say: I live in this world. And I am interested in your opinions. I ask you about these plays and movies, which I see, which you see . . .

Petra   (*her expression reads 'I don't understand what you meant by "I come here"'*) You come here?

Man   Here. How can I . . . ?

Petra   Oh – it just gets me so angry. Drugs – drugs are not – violence, real violence, life, *life* – the poor, criminals, it is not – we romanticize it – it is like – a drug – like – the trauma, the trauma of actually seeing this world is such that we create fantasies, we reward those who create *fantasies* because God forbid we look at – reality – at *ourselves* – there are people in this country, *other people* who are fascinating and, and *troubled* – and yet – where are they? – and New York and Los Angeles constantly dump this – shit this shit into this country, these people who are making these *things* who are desperate for – whatever – fame, money – and people will – eat it because they're hungry – these crumbs – and I don't – I'm not judging

those who watch or, or *read* this stuff – I watch it too
sometimes – but I blame those who – look – I am trying to
transcend – but there are pressures which prevent me – many
pressures and – I mean you say: you say, I come here. I say: I
work here.

Man   I come here . . . for fantasy. Is what I was going to say.
And what is so wrong with fantasy? If that's what we need to
live. Because. Don't we all have fantasies?

Petra   But there's a moral . . . in terms of art . . .

She stops.

I'm sorry.

Man   Here's the deal. I want you to show me your life.
Because it is so distant from my life. This is why I go to
movies, and plays. And come here. And so I know, I am
aware that perhaps you will find this – distasteful. Or immoral
even. But you would get to see my life. Which you, you could
not fathom. Where I work. The conversations I have. I am
asking for – some time – dinner, dates, you will take me to
coffee where you have coffee, I will take you to dinner where I
have dinner. I don't – I'm a gentle man – and I am a –
frightened man – and curious – and I don't – I know without
money I am nothing to you. I am a very rich person, and I
have herpes so I don't really have sex anymore.

Pause.

Petra   Let me ask you this. Why if you are interested in
getting to know somebody, in intimacy, why would you come
here? To a pornographic place?

Man   You're right. But I'll pay you not to come here. To
accompany me as though –

Petra   But why – in the first place – you're – you have
money – you're – nice – and attractive –

Man   Oh, come now. You tell me, how else might I have
met you. In a club? Come up to you in some club in Tribeca,
'Hey, how are you?'

Petra   But – I'm not talking about just me –

Man   I am. I find you fascinating. I don't find my secretary fascinating, I'm sorry.

Pause.

Petra   I work here, this is my job, I don't go home as this person I –

Man   Here.

He takes out a hundred-dollar bill and writes on it.

Now you can call me and. Call me and just. Talk to me about your life. And then. We can get together and have dinner and coffee a couple of times and I will pay you for your time. (*Rising.*) Take care, Petra.

He goes. She takes the hundred dollars.

Act Two

Scene One

Christmas Eve day. An apartment. **Darren** *is sitting on a sofa, flipping through some channels.* **Stephen** *is pouring and steeping tea. A lava lamp on a nightstand, red globs in yellow water.* **Darren** *has a slight, ambiguous, Britishy sounding accent.*

Darren I'm glad you called. I didn't know why you didn't call.

Stephen Oh, yeah. No I really liked you, I just, I was so overwhelmed and I've *been* so overwhelmed but lately I've just been feeling such a need to *connect*, things have been so – it's probably just the holidays, but. You know, God, these tea cups are gorgeous! I mean that's kind of a weird thing to say, but. Do you, sugar, or? Darren?

Darren Oh, yeah, just – this show. Yeah, an embarrassing amount of sugar. Yeah, that set was a thousand dollars, the cups and the plates and stuff.

Stephen *What?*

Darren Oh, that's right, you don't know – I sold a screenplay.

Stephen Oh, you did?

Darren Yeah, *and* made a deal to co-produce the sound-track. Three-hundred-thousand dollars against seven hundred.

Stephen Oh my God! Well that's extraordinary! Well – my God!

Darren Yeah, like four spoonfuls.

Stephen Okay. Well what's the screenplay about?

Darren Oh, you know, romantic comedy, East Villagers meeting cute, you know, stockbroker guy runs into squatter girl at ATM, blah blah blah the end.

Stephen   Well congratulations!

Darren   Are you still working on that play?

Stephen   Yeah, I am.

Darren   What's it about again?

Stephen   This incredible thing that happened in my hometown, this amazingly beautiful –

Darren   Where are you from again?

Stephen   Darien, Connecticut? Kind of, kind of upper-middle-class suburb, about an hour away.

Stephen *comes to the couch with the tea.*

Darren   So what are you doing for Christmas Eve tonight?

Stephen   Oh, um –

Darren   I have to make the rounds at these endless horrible parties. Then I have to go out to la-la land on the 26th, so it's kind of a truncated holiday.

Stephen   Right. Yeah, I'm not going home to my family, first time actually, that would just be self-loathing, and I have two friends in town so –

Darren   Do you like my lava lamp? I can't make up my mind about it.

Stephen   Oh – I don't like them in general. I always, I always thought they kind of looked like, I don't know, an abortion or something.

Darren   Really?

Stephen   Yeah.

Darren   That's kind of witty.

Stephen   Oh?

Darren   There's nothing on.

Stephen   So how's Maria?

Darren Maria?

Stephen What was her name? Marla?

Darren Magda, my friend Magda. Hey. I have something you'll like.

Darren *puts in a tape.*

Watch this.

He sits back on the couch.

Stephen God it's so nice to have a day off. Oh. Oh God.

Darren This is that homemade porno –

Stephen Oh.

Darren They *totally* wanted it released, I mean gimmie a break – I have a friend who gets all these, he got the, remember the Rob Lowe tape?, but that's pretty boring. This is *hot*. Look at how big Tommy Lee's dick is. That's a fucking beautiful cock, you have to admit.

Stephen Wow, it's really them. Pamela Anderson. Wow.

Darren *puts his hand in his pants, starts moving it around.*

Stephen Oh. Oh God you know. Maybe. I feel – I hope I didn't imply by just – calling up and coming over – that I wanted to –

Darren *unzips his fly, reaches in that way.*

Stephen You know, I think I'm gonna go.

Darren Aw, come on.

Stephen Yeah, I don't . . . I don't know. Yeah, I think I'm gonna go.

Darren Hey, I'll stop the tape. No big deal.

Stephen You know it's – I didn't, I just didn't expect you know – I hope I'm not – I just, I just –

Darren Do you have an erection?

Stephen   What?

Darren   I'm asking if you have a hard on. We'll just beat off.

Stephen   Well, I mean –

Darren   If you're not gonna answer me –

Darren *reaches for* **Stephen**'s *crotch.* **Stephen** *spills his tea.*

Stephen   Oh –

Darren   Ow! – You didn't have to spill the tea, Stephen – fuck! Ouch.

Stephen   I didn't mean to – my unconscious talking I guess.

Darren   Well why don't you leave before your unconscious breaks my VCR or my lava lamp.

Stephen   Good idea. Hah. Well my therapist will love hearing about this.

Darren   Okay.

Stephen   My jacket.

He gets his jacket, puts it on. **Darren** *goes off, into the bathroom. Water running.*

Stephen   You know, I was just, just hoping to talk, you know, about, just. Sorry. Okay. Well, hey, have a good Christmas.

Darren (*off*)   You too.

Stephen *hesitates. Touches his crotch, rubs. He looks off to the bathroom, looks quickly to the TV.*

Darren   Hello?

Stephen   Yeah, no, I'm going – I just – I'll call you when – I mean I like you I feel – it's not that I don't want to, to – I just –

Darren (*off*)   Okay, gotcha. Take care!

Stephen   You too!

Stephen *goes.*

Scene Two

A restaurant, fancy, conservative. Classical piano, far-off.

Man   So what are you doing after dinner. How are you spending your Christmas Eve?

Petra   Well, my two roommates are . . . we're exchanging gifts. And it's been a nightmare.

Man   What's going on?

Petra   Basically, my roommate Stephen's ex-lover, his name is Mark, had this big deal in Hollywood, started filming this movie, started doing a lot of drugs, then towards the end of it I guess basically had a nervous breakdown – so he went into rehab and became – found God more or less. And he's become friends with this street kid who's obviously unhealthy and on drugs and – he's ignoring Stephen, so. And this is very hard for Stephen to understand. So basically.

Man   Wow.

Petra   What?

Man   Fascinating. People. Their *lives*. My God.

Petra   What are *you* doing tonight?

Man   Nothing. Watch TV. Tomorrow I'm gonna drive to Connecticut and see my folks.

Beat.

What do you think of this restaurant?

Petra   It's lovely. I'm so excited for my monkfish.

Man   The monkfish, I've had it before. It's good.

Petra   I can't wait.

Man   Can I ask you a question?

Petra   Yes.

Man   And by the way, you look beautiful tonight. Stunning.

Petra   Thank you.

Man   Do your roommates tell you you're beautiful?

Petra   No.

Man   Well they should.

Petra   You're sweet.

Man   Why do you strip?

Beat.

Why do you keep – when obviously you don't have to.

Petra   Oh, is that obvious?

Man   Is it material? Do you get good material?

Petra   God, no.

Man   So it's really just. The money.

Petra   Well . . .

Man   New York City's so expensive.

Petra   Well, yes, but it's. Where. I feel I have to be.

Man   It's a big country.

Petra   But – here – the arts – that industry is . . . here. And I grew up here, to leave . . .

Man   I see these guys at the club. You put yourself through a lot of misery.

Petra   There's a lot – really – that I enjoy about dancing. A lot that I find fulfilling but. You know, office work is no less demeaning And yes, I do believe I learn, or see, have access to particular men, there's a rare intimacy about the setting . . .

Man   But it must make you crazy.

Petra   Crazy.

Man   You can tell me if I'm wrong.

Petra   I . . . enjoy it. Dancing I. It makes me feel good.

Man   Good how?

Petra   It makes me feel special.

Pause.

Man   I write poems sometimes, you know. (*Beat.*) Does that surprise you?

Petra   No.

Man   You want to be a writer, but I – well – I just dabble, nothing serious, just for me. See generally I run away. I go to a spa. I see a movie. Take a trip. That's what I do. But you. You walk head-first into it – your pain – every day. You have to, else you wouldn't be a writer.

Petra   No.

Man   No?

Petra   No, because pain – and consciousness – both are difficult but – I should hope there's a difference between the two. I think I am *conscious*. But pain – I don't want my pain any more than you want yours.

Man   See, that's what I – I mean, what *makes* you an artist? What happened to make you – I know how I got into investment banking, it's a pretty simple story. But you. This *person* you are, this *life*, what made you – how did it happen?

Petra   Okay. Okay.
I'm a freshman in college. A dorm, like a prison, falling apart, roaches, like rats in a lab we are, okay? My roommate is – Dominican or something – and one night she makes this big greasy pot of fish, in this very greasy yellow sauce, and she leaves it simmering on the stove. She goes out to meet her boyfriend. I go into the kitchen. I open the pot. Me. And it

looks like sewage. A huge – ridiculous this pot is. And I take out a spoon and think: I'll try this. And I do. I take another bite. Another. And I know, I am a rational being, I know she's cooked this for her boyfriend, they'll be back soon: the whole pot. All of it. And I run into the bathroom and I sit there I'm numb I put my hand into my mouth, okay? And I'm covered there in – fish – covered – I look – a ghoul – green, literally – and I'm thinking: *What?* Because I know enough to know this is not normal or healthy in any way and I want to know: *Why?* Why would I have done this: why do I feel this way? What in the world – literally, what in the world in which I find myself living, what at this point in history, what could make a person feel this unbearable sadness and think these terrible thoughts? These thoughts: *I will never be loved. I cannot live in this world.* You see? Because – because my roommate is going to come home and say Where is the fish and the only answer is Petra ate it. Petra ate the fish. And how can I go on? How can I go on without – and I know – that there are people who do not ask this question – because to know – is too much. Because society does not *afford* them the opportunity to know, and. Because they are in a constant state of *desire* and desire, *want*, inhibits consciousness. To become conscious you must stifle yourself, resist your impulses. Not that I had this language then. But I knew; I decided. I decided next time I would not eat the fish. No matter what. No matter what pain that caused me I would put the fork down and place the lid on the pot and.

Pause.

Man   What's your name?

Petra   My name is Petra.

Man   What's your real name?

Petra   My name is Petra.

Pause.

Man   Two years ago I bought my wife a necklace. For Christmas. Okay. She opened it up – she didn't like it. And I said, Well, it's okay, take it back. But I felt . . . angry. I felt . . .

sick. And then she stopped sleeping with me. Why? I didn't
know. And then I was on a trip. I met a woman in a bar. And
I had told myself many times that I would never . . . but I was
angry at my wife. I. Hated her. Despised – and so, and so I
had sex with this woman from the bar.
So what you're saying is.

Petra   Do you see? My story illustrates my awakening to
consciousness; yours does not. This is the difference – what I
was trying to say the other night – this is the difference
between art and pornography as well. Art can be ugly and
painful and full of disgusting things; but unlike pornography it
is *conscious* of this.

Man   Conscious or not, it's still . . . horrible. Horrible. Look
at . . . Woody Allen – the ways people behave – despite what
they know – I mean when did he decide, you know, to . . . ?
I'm not an intellectual man. I don't have words. Thank you,
Petra. Thank you for – you.

Pause.

Are you still in pain?

Petra   – No.

Man   I can't say I believe you, Petra.

Petra   No. No. I have beauty in my life. I have art, I have
friends –

Man   That's not what I asked.

They look at each other.

I can't wait for the food. This is the best food.

He sips from a glass of wine.

Scene Three

Apartment, that night. **Stephen** *arrives, entering with a bag.* **Mark***'s
on the phone, quickly hangs up.*

Stephen   Hey sweets!

Mark   Hi.

Stephen   Merry Christmas Eve. How are you?

Mark   I'm fine. How are you?

Stephen   Ugh shopping is *done!*

Mark   Good day?

Stephen   Great day! You?

Mark   Okay.

Stephen   How's Tan?

Mark   He hasn't come by.

Stephen   Oh? I hope he's all right.

Mark   Me too.

Stephen   So are you all ready for Christmas Eve?

Mark   Yes.

Stephen   Are you going to church?

Mark   Tomorrow morning.

Stephen   Oh, maybe I can go with you.

Mark   I don't think that's appropriate.

Stephen   Oh?

Mark   My faith is very special to me. I take it very seriously.

Stephen   Well – I'm not going to sit there making pedophile jokes about the priest.

Mark   I'm sorry. You understand.

Stephen   Well. Okay, whatever you need. I bumped into Petra at the deli, she'll be here in a couple of minutes.

Stephen *goes into his room, takes stuff out of the bags.*

So were you on the phone with Hollywood?

Mark   When?

Stephen   When I came in. You were on the phone.

Mark   No, I was thinking of calling someone.

Stephen   Oh. Hey, did you get the mail?

Mark   Yeah, you didn't get anything.

Stephen   Fuck.

Mark   I got something.

Stephen   Yeah?

Mark   They sent me the cut of the movie.

Stephen *re-enters the living room. Sees the large envelope atop the VCR.*

Stephen   The – your movie?

Mark   I need to make a decision by – it's going to be at Sundance – so they need to know. If I want. My name on it. I haven't – watched it yet.

Stephen   Wow . . . well, I'm sure that's going to be difficult for you.

Mark   What do you care about Tan?

Beat.

Stephen   Excuse me?

Mark   When you came in. 'How's Tan?'

Stephen   Are we all right here?

Mark   I mean just let me live my life don't. Judge me all the time.

Stephen   O-kay . . . is there . . . something you'd like to talk about?

Mark   How's Tan, Who were you on the phone with, I mean. Just – no – exactly – there is nothing about all this I'd like to talk to you about as long as you're *judging* me –

Stephen   All right, wait a second –

Mark   Your rage is so transparent and it's just toxic, you
know, it's poisoning this whole –

Stephen   Rage?

Mark   Yes, rage, at me, yes. I'm sorry we're not having sex,
I'm sorry this is so upsetting to you.

Stephen   *Mark?*

Mark   'How's Tan?'

Stephen   Okay, okay I'm not going to yell and, and also it's
Christmas Eve, but what I will say, what I will say is that you're,
you're really – hurting my feelings here. Okay? So just – so just
be a human being here for a second and let's go back to –

Mark   *What?*

Stephen   What? What?

Mark   What, I don't know how to be a human being now?

Stephen   That's not what I said.

Mark   What did you say then?

Stephen   Okay, let's take deep breaths –

Mark   Can you SHUT UP for a second? you're always
fucking TALKING.

Stephen   Shut – Mark – what – I ask how you are, I ask
about your life – you know if anyone should be angry here –
Jesus Fucking Christ! –

Mark   Oh, thank you.

Stephen   Oh, *oh*, excuse me for taking the fucking Lord's
name in vain, I'm sorry I'm not SPIRITUAL like you taking
you know fucking becoming intimate with a fucking STREET
KID hustler drug dealer whatever and you can't, you can't
even fucking find ten MINUTES to talk to me –

Mark   Stop yelling! –

Stephen   Stop – no! – you don't, you don't ask to even read what I'm working on, you sit here all day, *my* house, you invite this *kid* –

Mark   So you're jealous, because you think, you have some *idea* –

Stephen   Well I'm sorry if I'm a little fucking cynical I mean where's, how are you being a good Christian all this religious BULLSHIT, I mean, go fucking pass out food to smelly ugly homeless men, don't give me this Christian shit about – being –

Mark   Stop yelling!

Stephen   – no, go deliver food to people dying of AIDS, go, fuck you –

Mark   STOP YELLING!

Pause. **Mark** *beginning to cry.*

Stephen   Oh – come on – don't – don't – why are you – don't cry –

Mark   You know I was – I was – away for a long time I wasn't in the world and – I'm *adjusting* you know and it's not – I'm doing the best I – it's hard and you could show some – compassion –

Stephen   Come on, don't cry –

Mark   – because – I just wanted – a safe space and – you fucking accuse me of – all this judging, all this – let he who is without sin cast the first – you know? – I never said I was – perfect and I'm sorry if I'm not who – you wanted – me – to be – anymore –

Stephen   No, that's not – come on, don't cry. That's not it. I'm sorry, I shouldn't have – yelled I.

Mark *breaks down.* **Stephen** *puts his arm around him.*

Stephen   I just – if you're in pain I want to – it's – shhhh, come on. Shhh. It's okay. Shhh.

Mark   I have to go to the bathroom.

Mark *gets up, goes to the bathroom off. Door opens.* **Petra**.
Stephen *picks up the phone, pushes a button.*

Petra   Hey!

Stephen   Hi.

Petra   Who are you talking to?

Stephen   Shhhh.

Stephen *listens. Then gasps.*

Petra   What?

Stephen *hangs up.*

Petra   Is Mark home?

Toilet flushes. **Mark** *enters, not crying.*

Petra   Hey sweetie!

Mark   Hey Pet.

Mark *goes over to* **Petra**, *gives her a big hug and a kiss.*

Petra   Okay boys. Are you ready for something?

Stephen   Uh-oh.

Petra   Look what I *bought* myself for *Christmas* – can you guess?

Stephen   What is it?

Petra   Okay, get ready . . .

She opens her bag and removes: a bagel. She laughs hysterically.
Stephen *and* **Mark** *laugh with her.*

Scene Four

*Apartment. Trees are decorated. Some presents and wrapping paper scattered.
Laughter. Christmas music playing softly.* **Petra** *has her arm around*
Mark. **Stephen** *sits across from them. Occasionally* **Petra** *runs her*

hand through **Mark***'s hair. The large envelope is still atop the TV.*

Petra   No, I have another one. Even worse.

Stephen   Okay, wait, neither of you knows this one. I am at an audition for a play, this is back like three years ago, and it was a serious play, you know, really heady stuff, and I'm standing outside the room waiting, and we were to wait in this hallway while the auditions were going on, and I'm standing outside the room waiting, whatever, and I hear the actor giving his reading, of the sides. And I got a little startled and nervous because it was a very good reading, really unique and unorthodox but honest and risky, and suddenly my reading seemed so conventional. So he leaves, and he's this striking blond man, glowing eyes, very, that kind of ethereal beauty – and I say hey and he says hey and he goes down the stairs, and I'm waiting: I can hear the casting directors talking – the door to the room is made of this really cheap wood, it's like, cork or something, right? So I hear this older man's voice, middle-aged, and I hear him say, 'My God, I could fuck that boy a thousand ways to Sunday. My *God*.' You know. And this woman laughs and says 'He is *ohhhh*' and I hear the man say, 'And he is *stacked* beneath those clothes, I can tell.' And I hear someone else laugh. And, and then I hear footsteps, the door opens for me, and I go in, and there they are: poker-faced. And I say hi, and I meet the reader, some effeminate twenty-three year old, the third person I heard laughing. And I do my reading, very good, blah blah blah, good job, nice to see you, Stephen. But all I'm thinking, I'm leaving and I'm thinking, and I couldn't stay to listen to what they said obviously, there's another actor there now, but I'm walking down the stairs onto horrible west 42nd street and it's cold and the only thought in my mind is: Did he want to fuck me a thousand ways to Sunday? Nothing about my audition, my reading, my talent, my choices, no, all I could think was: did he wonder what I looked like under my clothes? And I felt soft and miserable. And went to the gym. For about a week. But. Like. I mean – it was all I cared about, would that fat fifty-year-old jerk off to my headshot that night?

Petra   Because what can you do in that situation? You want the role! It's a good play so how do you not become, in some way, the person they want you to be? You have to be a Zen Master not to want him to masturbate onto your headshot!

Mark   How we treat people – sometimes makes them what they are.

Stephen   God – you know? Who are these people? How do they sleep at night? Shame on them! Oh!

Petra   People, my God.

What about you, sweetie? You have any horror stories? My God, this is such a catharsis for me, it's such a release hearing all this stuff.

Mark   Um. Well. Yeah, I.

Petra   Oh yeah? Good.

Mark   When I was um. Making my film, about two weeks before my, whatever, my, you know . . . okay: I'm just gonna try to – tell this. Okay. Deep breath, wow. Okay. So. We all went out after the shoot and basically started off by getting drunk before we moved on, you know, to everything else. And. I sat there with my actors and. This one, Adam, said to the group, said. *Mark fucks like a Calvin Klein ad.* Out of. The blue and. Adam had a small role, and the actors didn't know him too well but he was my friend so. He'd come out with us. We'd been talking about how many people we'd. Slept with. Was the topic of conversation and. I'd found myself *inflating*. Because I was embarrassed at how, comparatively, how *few*. Anyway. The actors look at him and. I say. What can I say? *That was a long time ago.* Not even a year, Adam says. And the actors start *laughing*. Well. *What do you mean by that?* And Adam says. *I mean he has this vacant stare which never changes.* And I. Smile. And I say. *Adam you never open your eyes during sex so how would you know.* And.

Mark *starts to cry a little.* **Petra** *grabs his hand.*

Mark   It was just then that I. I realized I. Well. So I

laughed. We all laughed and. That night another actor came
to my room at the hotel we. In West Hollywood, a nice, the
Mondrian, we were there for two nights while we were filming
in L.A. And this actor came in and. Went in and turned on
the shower and said. We're gonna take a shower and fuck and
I have some Percosets for later my mom she went just went to
the dentist and. And. I did because.

He stops the story. And stops crying. And laughs. And then silence.

Because, you know. Because I thought . . .

He waves his hand, as if to signal that he won't go on. **Stephen** *grabs
a small wrapped flat gift.*

Stephen   Here, here, last one.

Petra   Ooooh.

Stephen   For you, Mark.

Mark   You got me another gift? Wow.

Stephen   Well, it's a little self-serving because it's for both of
us, but –

He hands **Mark** *a small envelope.* **Mark** *opens it, takes out two
tickets.*

Mark   Oh, wow.

Stephen   It's supposed to be really good, it was a hit in
London or whatever, so, and it's in previews now, and I
thought. We used to have so much fun going to plays together,
that used to be our thing, so. I thought it would be nice. And
we could go eat after at Leshko's like we did when we had no
money. And the only difference would be that we didn't have
to usher to get in, or get TKTS or whatever.

Mark   Great.

Stephen   Yeah, so.
Hey. Three minutes to Christmas! Eleven-fifty-seven . . .
now!

Mark   Thank you. It's on New Year's Eve.

Stephen   Yes. There's this, someone was telling me about some culture which believes in spending New Year's Eve in a ritualized, like, in this way where everything you do you do in hopes that your year will follow in that fashion. So if you want a year of clarity, you spend the evening cleaning your home, – you make it symbolic and – so I just thought going to a play, karma-wise, might be a really nice, low-key way

The buzzer buzzes.

Huh?

Petra   Who in God's name?

Stephen *answers with intercom.*

Stephen   Hello?

Tan (*off/through intercom*)   Hey uhh – Mark?

Stephen *looks to* **Mark**.

Tan   Mark, come down! It's Tan!

Mark *stands.*

Mark   I suppose I should . . . go see him for a minute . . . I guess.

Stephen   Oh, okay.

Mark *grabs his coat and his sketchpad.*

Petra   I hope he's all right.

Mark   I'll be back.

Mark *goes to the door, gets his coat.* **Petra** *starts collecting wrapping paper.* **Stephen** *goes to* **Mark**.

Stephen   Hey, are you going to be all right?

Mark   Yeah.

Stephen   I'm sorry about earlier.

Mark   It's okay.

Stephen   Anything you need, you know.

Mark   I know.

Stephen   If you're out just call – if you want to talk when you get back – just knock on my door.

Mark   Thanks a lot. Bye.

Stephen   See you later.

Mark *exits, door slams.*

Petra   That kid is bad news, I hope he knows what he's doing.

Stephen   Well listen to this. We got into a little tiff before you got home – and he – you won't believe this – and I grabbed the phone because he had been on it when I came home, and I just hit the re-dial, and wouldn't you know – no, guess. Guess who he's talking to.

Petra   Ethan Hawke, how the hell do I know.

Stephen   Phone sex.

Petra   Oh.

Stephen   He's. A fucking mess is what he is. He said he's – whatever. Merry Fucking Christmas, Mark. I mean, what can I do?

Petra   Well . . . you can –

Stephen   It's not fair. He can't be honest with me? I love him. I love him and I've done nothing except try to help him. This Bible shit.

Petra   Maybe that's what he needs, Stephen.

Stephen   These stupid recovery programs!

Petra   Why are they stupid?

Stephen   Because they turn people into – all that *shit* about 'That was some other person who was addicted, that was not me' and 'God give me the strength'. So he can't talk to me but he can call phone sex, FUCK him!

Petra   He's a recovering drug addict. He must be –

Stephen   What, is this another I'm OK You're OK no, no, I am *fine* and *he* is fucked up, so, so I'm being judgmental, well, so *fine*, I think I'm allowed I think that's IN FACT I think it's *important*.

Petra   Okay, calm down. I think you should try to understand that –

Stephen   And he actually gave me that line, let he who is without sin, Christ I just LOVE how faggots lay that one on you, how many times do I have to hear some morally vacant FUCK say that?! And, and he buys me a BIBLE for Christmas! A Bible! Whooo!

Petra   It's just his way of telling you who he is now. He's sharing –

Stephen   – yeah –

Petra   Try to be selfless, take a step back and you'll see –

Stephen   Selfless? What, am I a therapist? No, I – I let him – I love him – I LOVE HIM – and he's – who the fuck knows what he's doing – he could be – you know? –

Petra   I'm not on his side, I'm just trying –

Stephen   Oh no, well what's with, with all this, this hands all over him always hugging him, what the hell is that?

Petra   I don't understand.

Stephen   I mean, there you are, I mean, what about me? Who's holding my hand? Who's hugging me? And where's my two-million-dollar three-picture deal?

Petra   I think you have to ask yourself why you're so upset, Stephen.

Stephen   Because I am, and I'm allowed to be fucking upset, so – so fuck you too!

Stephen *picks up some wrapping paper, puts it into the garbage, goes to his room, shuts the door. Climbs into bed. Petra looks around. She takes a small gift and unwraps it. It's her bagel. She sits on the couch and takes a bite of it.*

Scene Five

A luxurious bathroom. A huge, white circular bathtub; gray mottled walls. Gleaming chrome fixtures. Mirrors. A bathroom at the Royalton Hotel.

Tan   It's cool, isn't it.

Mark   It's really beautiful. So peaceful. Clean.

Tan   I swear to God. He books the room an extra night and leaves, lets me have it. Like once a month. Isn't that weird?

Mark   And all he leaves is dirty underwear?

Tan   He leaves them under the bed. And they're smeared – you know, cum, shit, piss. You know. But – I tell him I jerk off onto them and then I mail them back to him. He leaves the envelope, already stamped and shit. But I don't jerk off onto them, and he can't tell the difference.

Mark   Sick.

Tan   So I just come and take a bath. Sometimes I order porno. They have that Simon Rex jerk-off tape, *Young Hard and Solo 2*.

Mark   Do they?

Tan   And I order a Black Angus. Mmmmmm.

Mark   Wow.

Tan   We can eat whatever. Just charge it to the bill. Guy's loaded. I met him by jerking off for him. And he always leaves a couple hundreds hid somewhere. In the room, you know. He draws little pictures on the bills. Little smiley faces.

Mark   Wow.

Tan   Beat off for him in Times Square, on 41st Street. Three a.m.

Mark   No cops?

Tan   You'd be surprised. How easy it is to do things and no one notices. I've had cops walk ten feet away and not even see.

Beat.

So we gonna take a bath together or what?

Mark   Tan.

Tan   I love how you say my name. Gives me a boner.

Mark   Yeah?

Tan   See for yourself. Bathtub! Wheee!

Tan *leaps into the empty bathtub. Only his head and shoulders are visible.*

Mark   There's such a light about you, you know. Underneath everything, you have this joy . . .

Tan   You could fit your whole bathroom in this tub.

Mark   I'm – just not – sure what's happening here, Tan.

Tan   Neither am I!

Tan *tosses his shoes out of the tub.*

Wheeee!

Mark *laughs.*

Tan   They give you free bubble bath.

Tan's *belt comes ripping off.* **Mark** *stares away, at mirror.*

Mark   Well, I guess I wonder why. I wonder why you're here and why. Why you don't. Go somewhere for help You're. So young and. You know? It's wrong for me to. Well just in terms of me I shouldn't – my heart is starting to – hurt and. But. You should get help and if I can.

Tan *laughs. Pants over the edge of the tub. Socks. Underwear.* **Tan** *giggles.* **Mark** *laughs.*

Mark   Okay.

Tan *takes off his shirt.*

Mark   Well. Do you. Do you have anything to say about what I'm. Saying or?

Tan *stands, back to us, naked. Reaches, dims the light.* **Mark** *looks in the mirror, then closes his eyes.*

Mark   Look I.

He opens his eyes, keeps them vaguely averted.

I got you a Christmas gift, and then I'm going to leave, okay? But I wanted to give you . . .

Mark *puts his sketchpad on the bathtub.*

Tan   Don't go. I got you something too.

Tan *opens the pad.*

Wow, it's your drawings.

Oh wow.

Is that me?

Mark   Yes.

Tan   (*flipping through*) Oh wow.

Mark   Yes.

Tan   Wow.

Mark   You can jerk off if you want to.

Tan   What?

Mark   Okay. And then I'll leave. Okay?

Tan   Okay.

Mark   Lay down. In the tub.

Tan *does. We can't see him.* **Mark** *watches in the mirror.*

Tan   Can you see?

Mark *nods.*

Tan   I like you watching.

Mark   Open your legs a little.

Tan   Makes me feel good.

Mark *watches.*

Scene Six

Apartment. **Stephen**'s *asleep in his bed.* **Petra**'s *at the kitchen table, reading.* **Mark** *enters.*

Petra   Hi.

Mark   Hi. Can I talk to you?

Petra   Sure.

Mark   Is Stephen asleep?

Petra   I think so.

Mark   Come here.

Mark *sits on his couch, wraps himself in a blanket.* **Petra** *comes over, sits on the edge of the couch. He doesn't say anything. He snuggles into her a bit.*

Petra   Are you all right?

Mark   You won't tell Stephen what I tell you will you?

Petra   Well. No.

Mark   Promise. He'll be mad.

Petra   Are you all right?

Mark   Yeah. No. No I'm not all right. Will you say a prayer with me?

Petra   Sure.

Mark   My heart is just. I have to make all these – I almost – I almost – with Tan tonight – I just – what can I do about my heart? My heart feels like . . . oh God. I hurt. I *hurt*. What can I do? What can I do?

Petra   I think it's –

Mark   Read, read this.

He hands her some wrinkled pieces of paper.

Petra   What . . . is this . . .

Mark   It's. Tan wrote a comic book. See. He gave it to me. For Christmas.

Petra   Oh my God. What? Oh my God.

Mark   (*as* **Petra** *flips through the pages*) In the first panel there that's – it's his mother – on this public toilet – at some – seedy – bar. There's no words, you know, and he explained it to me in this, this – like – recounting the plot of a *Seinfeld* – and then – his mother – is on the toilet because she's having her period so she – ovulates – drops the egg – and leaves – and then his father comes into the bathroom and goes – defecates – and then – doesn't flush but looks and sees the – feces and – the blood there and – masturbates into the toilet – and – the conception – he flushes – and the fetus grows – in the sewer – and he develops, you see, there, with the alligators and then – and is born, finally – out of the sewer, nine months later, this pipe – into the East River.

Petra   Oh my.

Mark   I'm – I want – I want so bad to touch him, I almost – I almost –

Petra   You're shaking.

Mark   It feels – What can I do? – my heart –

Petra   I think Mark. I think the only thing for you to do is stop. Seeing him.

Mark   But he – he has nothing he needs me and –

Petra   He doesn't need you.

Mark   I've been so nice to him I can't – look he drew this and it's – beautiful but –

Petra   You don't need him and that's what you need to think about right now.

Mark   No.

Petra   That's – all I can say to you. You can't stop how you feel but you can change what you *do*.

Mark   It felt so good, Petra. It felt so good.

Petra   What? –

Mark   I used to use drugs I don't do that anymore I stopped.

Petra   I know you did and that was hard and I'm sure there was a time you never thought –

He puts his arm around her waist.

Mark   and I think I grew up and how –

Petra   I bet you thought it was impossible –

Mark   – and my heart. It felt so good. I don't feel good. I don't feel good.

Petra   Why don't we, Mark, why don't we say a prayer together.

Mark *moves away from her.*

Petra   Why don't we –

Mark   I need you to leave now.

Pause.

Petra   What?

Mark   You have to go please.

She sits up.

Petra   You want me to leave?

Mark   Yes.

Petra   Well. Okay.

Mark   I'm sorry.

Petra   I'll be in my room if you need anything.

Mark   Thank you.

Petra *goes, off.* **Mark** *stands. He goes to* **Stephen**'s *room. He climbs onto the loft bed. He shakes* **Stephen**.

Mark   Wake up.

Stephen *awakens.*

Stephen   Wha . . . ?

Mark   It's me.

Stephen   Wh – are you okay?

Mark   Hug me.

Stephen   Mark?

Mark *climbs atop* **Stephen** *and hugs him.*

Stephen   Are you – okay? –

Mark   Shhh.

Mark *keeps hugging. Then starts rubbing against* **Stephen**.

Stephen   Whoa –

Stephen *sits up, pushes* **Mark** *away.*

Mark   What?

Stephen (*still groggy*)   Mark, what?

Mark   Hug me again. Just hug.

Stephen   Mark – are you okay?

Mark   You said I needed anything I could wake you up.

Stephen   I know –

Mark   I was remembering us – how good it felt –

Stephen   Well – yeah –

Mark   – so just hug me Stephen hug me

Stephen   Oh God.

Mark   What?

Stephen   Oh God oh.

Stephen's *face tightens.*

Mark   What? What?

A beat.

Stephen (*flustered*)   I – I came.

Mark   You came?

Stephen   I – Mark –

Mark   You came without? – But you weren't touching yourself –

Stephen   I – I know I

Mark   I want to come.

Stephen   Mark –

Mark   I want to come now.

Stephen   Mark, please – oh God, please let's leave my bed –

Mark   Are you – come on I want to come, you just came –

Stephen   What's – what's wrong?

Mark   Stephen!

Stephen   Let's just go into the living room.

Mark   One night, once, Stephen,

Mark *buries his head in* **Stephen**'s *chest, kisses, fumbles with his jeans.*

Stephen   No, Mark, no, Mark, we can talk, we can talk –

He pushes him away.

Mark   I don't want to talk! I'm sick of I don't want to talk!

Stephen   Mark I want to help you I want –

Mark *jumps off the bed.*

Mark   I'm leaving, I'm leaving.

Stephen *climbs off the bed.*

Stephen   Mark you shouldn't go out –

Mark   I didn't touch him, I didn't do anything with him Stephen –

Stephen   You stay here, I'll go.

Mark   What are you doing? Go where?

Stephen   Just stay here.

Mark   Where are you –

Stephen *goes to the closet, takes clothes, begins putting them on.*

Where are you going?

Stephen. Stephen. Stephen! Don't – where are you going? You can't leave. Stephen – answer me! – don't fucking leave me Stephen. Don't leave me here –

Mark *blocks* **Stephen**'s *way.*

Mark   No. No.

Stephen *tries to go,* **Mark** *continues to block.* **Stephen** *pushes* **Mark** *out of the way, exits the bedroom. He puts on his shoes.*

Mark   Where are you going, answer me, answer me Stephen, Stephen answer me. Why aren't you ANSWERING me –

Stephen *grabs his backpack. He begins to cry.*

Mark   Stephen – Stephen – I need you right now where are you – come back here! Come back here! Come *back* here!

Stephen *puts on a coat, still crying.*

Mark   Don't – cry Stephen. Okay. Okay. Look I'm quiet now. Look I'm quiet. I'm okay. You don't know what happened. We can talk about it. We can talk about what happened. We can talk just please don't. Come back to bed. Come back.

Stephen *gets his keys, goes to the door.*

Mark   It's late, Stephen, where – it's Christmas. It's Christmas. It's Christmas. It's.

Stephen *opens the door.*

Mark   Stephen. Stephen!

Stephen *goes. Door slams.*

Mark   Stephen! –

Stephen *begins punching his leg. He stops. His face is blank. His breathing is heavy.* **Petra** *comes out of her room, listens. Silence.* **Mark** *walks to the couch.* **Petra** *quickly sneaks back into her room.* **Mark** *takes the cordless phone and goes back to* **Stephen**'s *bed. He dials, presses the phone to his ear, curls into a fetal position.*

Act Three

Scene One

Petra *sits on the couch reading.* **Stephen** *comes storming in.*

Stephen Hi.

Petra When did you get back?

Stephen This morning. So listen. I got fired.

Petra Oh no.

Stephen Yes because. Because someone, because I made up, I wrote the blurb for *Men In Black* without watching it, they *found* out, someone *told* them. Someone, I told some *intern* in the office who I guess *blabbed* it. And literally. They called me into the office and asked me if I'd watched the movie. And. And you know. What am I? – I laugh. I laugh. Because. I say, 'Well,' because I did watch the trailer, I watched the trailer so – so – I mean, come on! So they said, and there's two of them there, my boss and the 'other' boss, the boss I never see, you know, the one who's always out having *lunch* eight hours a day. So what am I going to say, Yes, I did watch it and what, take a POP QUIZ on *Men In Black*?

Petra So what did you say?

Stephen I said I – *fast-forwarded* through it. And they said *That is not good enough.* And I said *Okay.* I'm sitting there. And they said *We're sorry.* And they sent me to *personnel.* And I have credit card bills, you know, this is not – I'm a – walking down the street. I write blurbs. I am a blurb writer. And you know, I didn't want to watch *Men In Black* that day, you know, and – you would think they'd – find it *funny*. But. So. So. New Year's Eve, here we are. Thank *God* this year is behind me is all I have to say. *Whooosh.* Goodbye.
Any word from Mark?

Petra I haven't seen him.

Stephen   Well, I guess that's it. I guess I'm going to the play alone tonight. Unless you want to . . .

Petra   I can't, I have – I made some plans.

Stephen   Have you seen him at all since I went home?

Petra   He's been here a lot during the day. On the phone.

Stephen   Have you been talking to him?

Petra   No. Listen you got –

Stephen   Did I do the right thing? That night was just so – maybe I shouldn't have gone home, maybe I should have *stayed* and just forced him to talk . . . his stuff's still here . . .

Petra *hands* **Stephen** *an envelope.*

Stephen   Oh God.

Petra   This is it?

Stephen   This is it. This came today?

Petra   Mm-hmm.

He opens it. He takes out the letter.

Stephen   I got it. I, yeah, I got it. Oh my God. I got it, seven-thousand dollars.

Petra   Oh. Yes. Yes.

Stephen   Thank you. Oh my God. Wow! Oh God. That's great. Oh my God.

Petra   Oh, I'm so happy for you.

Stephen   Wow.
Wow! Well that's over. I got it. Done.
Oh.

Stephen *grabs the large envelope from the top of the TV.*

Stephen   Look.

Petra   What?

Stephen   He still hasn't opened it.

He puts it back on the TV. He looks at his grant letter again. **Petra** *looks at him and smiles.*

Scene Two

A sleek modern apartment. **Man** *and* **Petra**.

Man   Before we go any further, I want to get this out of the way.

He hands her an envelope. She puts it into her purse.

Now. Now that that's done I want you to know – you can leave anytime you want. Okay?

Petra   Okay.

Man   So. This is it. I know, it could use a woman's touch.

Petra   It's very minimalist.

Man   Well that's not really by design. My wife kept all the really great stuff. Have a seat.

She sits on a couch.

Do I have plans for us tonight. What's better than a quiet New Year's at home?

Petra   It's such a difficult holiday to do right.

Man   You're telling me! Misery of miseries! I've never had a good New Year's Eve.

Petra   You're kidding! Oh God, me either. There's not one New Year's Eve where I haven't cried.

Man   Well, not tonight. That's the only rule, okay? Now: wine?

Petra   I'd love a glass.

He pours wine.

Man   So first off the bat, tell me how you are.

Petra   I'm okay. Stephen got back today. He got that grant which is very exciting.

Man   Do you realize that whenever I ask how you are, you tell me about someone else?

Pause.

Petra   I'm well, thank you.

Man   I want this to be a good holiday for you. A good New Year's Eve.

Petra *sips wine.*

Man   Tell me what you're writing. Tell me what you've been working on, how about that.

Petra   Well, I've been reading a lot. This excellent book by Mary Gaitskill; and Dorothy Parker, who's very underrated I think. People dismiss her as some sort of alcoholic, you know, little funny poem writer, but. She wrote some devastating fiction. The class issues are . . .

Man   Maybe you can lend me her book.

Petra   Yes.
Listen. I. I don't want to take your money. Not tonight.

Man   Anyway. Listen. I want to read you a poem.

Petra   I'm serious –

Man   Not now. Here.

Petra *sips wine.*

Man   Okay. This isn't easy. Okay.

'The darkness of your eyes
pierces into my heart.
I cannot fathom the size
of the waters you part.
You contain such light
that I cannot even see.
But I shall take flight
in your utter beauty.'

There. I said it.
Okay. Be honest. Tell me. I know, rhyming's kind of passé,
right?

Petra   I'm – very glad you wrote that. I hope. I hope it gave
you some joy.

Man   It's about you.

Petra   That . . . makes me feel good.

The man smiles.

Scene Three

The apartment. **Stephen**'s *sitting, reading.* **Mark** *enters.*

Mark   Hi.

Stephen   Hi. Are you . . . the play starts in half an hour, are
you? . . .

Mark   Oh no. I have this – party to go to. I'm – sorry, I
forgot all about it.

Stephen   Well – we haven't spoken since – so . . . I um – I
should get going but I thought –

Mark   I just came to pick something up.

Mark *crosses to the large envelope atop the TV, takes it.*

   . . . Are you going to the play alone?

Stephen   Yeah.

Mark   Cool. You went home to see your folks Pet said, how
um. How was that?

Stephen   It was good. Actually. As good as . . . you know.

Mark   Yeah. Well.

Stephen   Right.

Mark   Happy New Year's.

Stephen   You too.

Mark *goes. Door slams.* **Stephen** *crosses to his jacket. He puts it on. He goes to the door. He waits some moments. And goes.*

Scene Four

The Royalton bathroom. They've set a TV and VCR up on the sink counter. **Mark** *and* **Tan** *are watching, passing a cigarette between them. They sit in the giant tub. We can see they are bare chested.*

Sounds from TV.

Tan   Man. Yeah. Yeah.

Mark   Hah. Yeah, I shot that, that was fun.

Tan   What was he like, in real life?

Mark   He was whatever.

Mark *uses an eye-dropper to drop a few darkish drops of liquid into his nose. He hands the eye-dropper to* **Tan***, who gives him the cigarette.*

Tan   This is totally cool, man.

Mark   Yeah. I feel good. I feel good.
Did I tell you about the bathroom in the place I looked at? Practically identical to this one . . . 'cept not mirrors like these but . . .

Tan (*finishing with the drops*)   You know what I was thinking.

Mark   What?

Tan   I was thinking it'd be cool to come, you know, as the clock hits twelve or whatever.

Mark   Yeah?

Tan   Yeah. You don't think that's cheesy do you?

Mark   No. I think it's kind of hot.

Tan   Yeah.

Tan *takes* **Mark***'s hand with the cigarette, brings it to his mouth,* *inhales. Lets go.*

Tan   Whoa! Butch camera angle! Fuck! That dude, what's his name? He's cool.

Scene Five

Man's *apartment.* **Petra**'s *a little tipsy.*

Petra   You know what people want? I'll tell you, you, me, Quentin Tarantino, Bill Clinton, whether they know it or not, I'll tell you exactly what people want: love. As stupid as that sounds.

Man   Hah, you're getting drunk, I've never seen you like this.

Petra   No, we're all the same, in this, in just this one way, look: look: they have on videotape of, they have children, they did this in Britain, this study, okay, and little kids would get beaten up by their mothers, little, two-and three-years-old, slapped, punched, disgusting – but when the nurse came into the room – they actually did this, secret videotape – when the nurse came in to stop the beating and take the baby from the abusive mother, the baby cried, the baby cried and tried to hang on to its mother. So. So whatever you want to call it, that's – the baby wants – love – so the love is inappropriate, so what, it's what the baby knows . . .

Man (*laughing*)   And some babies grow up to make movies and run countries.

Petra *laughs, refills her wine glass.*

Man   You sure about that?

Petra   I'm not drunk. Okay. You asked me once, you said are you in pain? And I lied. I said no. And I'm in pain because I am not loved. You see. And artists – there's so little love to go around – the promise of love is so fleeting and inconsistent so to get noticed – people do – what they *do* is – just like you cheated on your wife, you see it in art too, the terror of not being loved, safe art, meaningless art, pandering art, commercial art, titillating art, outrageous art, can we sell it, can I sell myself, will I be rewarded with money, with prestige, with recognition – all those things which are, which are *perversions* of love - and let me tell you. If there were more love to go around. And more consciousness and less fear. People might make beautiful things. Beautiful things. What are all these horrible disgusting movies with violence and anger and, you know, I mean, they're cries for help! You look at a Quentin Tarantino movie, you know, This man has never been loved. He has had no experience of love in his life. Art, the art can never be better than the person who made it.

Man   Well you have to love yourself, don't you? Isn't that the hardest part?

Petra   You know what? That's New Age bullshit. You can't love yourself. You go and try. One is a fiction. Reality exists when the other person walks into the room. Life is other people.

Man   So is hell, or so someone said.

Petra   Well then so is heaven.

Man   Do you think you'll be loved?

Petra   I'd better.

Man   Do you think you will?

Petra   Hey, if I didn't, I'd put my head in the oven.

Man   Me too. Hah. That calls for one more glass I think. We're not even close to the ball dropping you know.

Man *pours himself a drink.* **Petra** *gets up, goes to a rack of CDs.*

Petra   Okay, tell me you have more than Bob Dylan.

Man   Van Morrison.

Petra   Shut up, what do you have to dance to?

Man   Oh God. Dance?

Petra   Yeah, you're gonna dance with me.

Man   Dance.

Petra   Here we go.

Petra *puts on a slow, sexy Janet Jackson song. She starts to dance.*

Man   Wow, look at you.

Petra   Come on, get up here.

He does.

Man   I can't believe I'm doing this.

He starts to dance. **Petra** *laughs.*

Petra   See! You're great!

Man   Don't mock me!

Petra   You're great!

Petra *moves closer to* **Man***, dances.*

Come on, just let go.

Man   That's very hard for insecure people.

Petra   You're good! God I love dancing.

Man   You do, eh.

Petra   The only orgasms I've had, the last two years – while I've been dancing.

Man   You're joking.

Petra   Only when I've been dancing. And I've been in plenty of beds in that time.

Man   Really, when you're stripping?

Petra   Mm-hmm. See, now you're dancing!

Man   Don't condescend.

Petra   I'm not. Here, you have to look at the person when you're dancing.

Petra *grabs him and slow dances.*

Man   Whoa.

Petra   When's the last time you danced?

Man   My wedding night I think.

Petra   So you don't have herpes, do you?

Man *stops a little, then starts up again.*

Man   Well why do you ask?

Petra   Answer the question, come on.

Man   No. No I don't. Have it.

Petra *laughs. They dance.*

Man   Nothing gets by your artist's eye, does it?

Petra   I want to go to your bed.

Man   You want to go to my bed?

Petra   Yes.

Man   No you don't.

Petra   Yes I do.

Man   Well I don't want to.

Petra *smiles, dances a few steps longer, then stops.* **Man** *stops.*

Man   I mean – you're gorgeous but. But. That's not right. You shouldn't – maybe you had a little too much to drink –

Petra   You know, I'm not a child, three, four glasses of wine, I am *conscious*. It's not like I popped a Rohypnol too.

Man   I'm sorry.

Petra   You're sorry? You're – fuck you.

Man   Whoa, what?

Petra   Fuck you you're sorry you – you invite me to your apartment and – New Year's Eve – and you tell me I'm beautiful and you write a –

Man   Wait, I never said – I never, I was always up front –

Petra   No, you manipulative you, no you made me – you made me – no –

Man   – about what I wanted, I was always honest with you. I was always. Here. Sit. Sit. You're drunk.

Petra *sits back down.*

Man   I'm sorry.

Oh God.

She takes a deep breath.

Listen. Listen I just wanted to talk to you. I just – I never wanted this to –

She stands.

Petra   You know what, I'm just gonna go home.

Man   Are you sure?

Beat.

Petra   Yeah. Yeah I'm sure.

Man   I'll talk to you . . .

Petra   Well, look at us. Look at this, you know.

Pause. **Man** *goes to the stereo, shuts off the music.*

Man   You – you should be having a blast. I wanted you to have a good New Year's Eve. I'm sorry.

Petra   No, this is. This *is* a good New Year's Eve. Actually. If you can believe it.

Petra *laughs.*

Man   Let me call you a car.

She reaches into her pocketbook and takes out the envelope.

Petra   Look, I can't, and I don't want to, take this.

Man   No. No. You. I think you're valuable. I value you and you. You should go out there and. Make something beautiful.

She looks at him. She puts the envelope back in her pocketbook.

Petra   You're gonna make me cry.

Man   No! Don't cry! Listen, let me call you a car.

He goes to the phone, across the room.

Hi, I need a car at 178 East 72nd Street. Yes. To the East Village. Yes.

Petra *begins to cry, silently.*

Man   To um – what's the street address? Petra?

Petra   – 199 East 4th.

Man   To 199 East 4th. Yeah, 178 East 72nd. Thanks!

He hangs up.

They'll be right there.

She turns. She walks to him and gives him a hug.

Oh – oh – you're crying.

Petra   I'm okay.

Man   You're sure?

Petra   Yeah.

She lets go. Laughs, wipes away tears.

God, my accent comes out so bad when I cry.

A beat.

Man   I am gonna watch me some Dick Clark tonight.

They share a brief laugh.

The car'll be right down.

Petra *nods.*

Petra   Goodbye.

Man   I'll uh – I'll keep an eye out for you. In the papers, I mean. I don't imagine I'll be seeing you – at the club. So. I'll. Good luck with everything.

Petra   Thank you. You too.

Petra *goes.*

Scene Six

The Royalton bathroom. Post-coital, on the tile floor.

Mark   Oh God.

Tan   You fuck like someone who hasn't fucked in a really long time.

Mark   Yeah well. Before this . . . it was a really long time.

Tan   You're good.

Mark   You too.

He kisses **Tan** *on the head.*

Mark   I'm cold. I'm gonna put on some clothes.

Tan, *naked, turns on the TV.* **Mark** *starts to dress.*

Tan   Hey dude, you're putting on my pants.

Mark   Oh yeah. Whoops. Oh well. See how I look.

He puts on the tight jeans. Really tight.

I'm Tan. Hello.

He takes **Tan***'s wallet out of his pants, opens it.*

Let's see here.

Tan   Whoa, whoa –

Mark *stops. Takes out a small card.*

Tan   – Well. Guess um.

Mark   You go to NYU?

Tan   Well, yeah. Yeah.

Tan *grabs a shirt –* **Mark**'s *– and throws it on.*

Mark   Huh.

Tan   Yeah, so.

He grabs pants, puts them on.

Mark   Whatever.

Mark *grabs* **Tan**'s *shirt, puts it on.*

Tan   What, you're not – mad?

Mark   No.

Tan   You're not?

Mark   I figured as much . . . I mean. It doesn't matter.

Tan (*face erupting into a smile*)   Really?

Mark   Yeah.

Tan   Hey you know I major, I major in acting.

Mark   Yeah?

Tan   Yeah, so, if you make any more movies . . .

Mark *smiles, nods, hands* **Tan** *his wallet. Looking at TV:*

Tan   Shit, it's ten minutes.

Mark   What?

Tan   Till the ball drops.

Mark   Oh.

Tan   We forgot. We finished too early.

Mark (*chuckles*)   Oops.

Tan   Wanna see if we can come? At midnight, we can try anyway? We can just, like, jerk off.

Mark   Um. Okay. What the hell.

Tan   'Cuz I think that'd be cool. To come at midnight.

Mark   Fun.

Tan   We could even do it by the window. People could see us. No one could tell who we were, and it'd be a kick, right?

Mark   Do it by the window?

Tan   And then people could see us.

Scene Seven

The apartment. **Stephen**'s *on the couch.* **Petra** *enters. We hear party noise from the street and from other apartments within the building.*

Petra   Hey.

Stephen   Why are you home? It's not midnight?

Petra   I'll be right back.

She goes into her room. Off:

I was thinking about what you said. About starting the New Year on a symbolic note. So I thought I'd come home and. Read or something.

Stephen   Oh. Well that's nice. I'm glad you're here.

Petra (*off*)   What?

Stephen   I'm glad you're here!

Some moments pass. **Petra** *comes into the living room, wrapped in a kimono. She sits on the couch.*

Stephen   Was your night okay?

Petra   Yeah.

Stephen   Yeah. Mine too.
I'm sad.

Petra   Me too.

Stephen   But it'll be okay.

Petra　Yeah. It'll be okay.

Pause.

Will you be mad at me if I leave, Stephen?

Stephen　Leave where?

Petra　If I leave here.

Stephen　You're going to leave?

Petra　I'm going to leave this city.

Stephen　You are?

Petra *nods.*

Stephen　Where are you going to go?

Petra　I don't know yet.

Stephen　When?

Petra　Soon.

Pause.

Stephen　Wow.

Petra　Yeah.

Stephen　You never said anything. When did you decide this?

Petra　I've been thinking about it for a long time.

Pause.

Stephen　I'll miss you.

Petra　I'll miss you.
How was the play?

Stephen *shrugs. Pause. Noise from outside.*

Stephen　What time is it?

Petra　Oh God, there's one minute.

Stephen　Eleven-fifty-nine.

Petra   Should we turn on the TV and watch all the people in Times Square and watch the ball drop?

Stephen   No.

Pause.

Petra   I'm gonna go read.

Pause. **Petra** *gets up, goes off to her room.* **Stephen** *stays seated.*

Outside, we hear continued sounds of people, shouting, honking, stomping around, screaming.

Stephen *does not move.*

We hear people counting down from ten.

Stephen *closes his eyes. The sounds increase.*

End.